INSIDE OUT:

An Incredible Journey

REXELLA VAN IMPE

Jack Van Impe Ministries
P.O. Box 7004, Troy, Michigan 48007
In Canada: Box 1717, Postal Station A
Windsor, ON N9A 6Y1

ISBN 1-884137-15-6

Book design by J. David Ford & Associates
www.jdavidford.com

Foreward

It is with great pleasure that I offer this introduction to Rexella's new book, taking you on a tour of her thoughts on vital subjects affecting our lives today. This "first lady" of Christian journalism, television, broadcasting, and vocal inspiration gives you her reflections in areas where you have ventured, but have hesitated to fully embrace. Truth must always be embraced — now or later.

Let this talented communicator lead you into God-given insights few people have been favored to receive. Rexella is a brilliant lady. She has earned multiple doctorates, and is respected as a genuine scholar. Her thoughts are keen, and her convictions are dear. The Bible is her ultimate guide and constant companion. We need to walk with her for a while through the pages of these articles, then we will see more clearly.

And then we will sense the Savior in a closer relationship.

In the Master's service,

Dr. Carl E Baugh
Dir. Creation Evidence Museum

Contents

Introduction

SIDE TRIPS
AND DETOURS

The saga of Joseph is one of my favorite stories in the Old Testament. An almost incredible account of twists and turns and ups and downs, truly his life was an incredible journey.

I'm sure you remember some of the details. He was the eleventh of twelve sons, and for a time was his father's favorite. Then one day out in the fields, his jealous brothers seized him, stripped off his coat of many colors, and threw him in a pit. While debating whether or not to kill him, a caravan of slave traders headed for Egypt came by and the brothers sold Joseph into bondage.

As a slave to an Egyptian army officer named Potiphar, Joseph soon became an esteemed and valued servant, entrusted with the management of the household. Then the officer's wife tried to seduce him. When he refused her advances, she accused him of rape—and Joseph was sent to prison.

As a prisoner, Joseph quickly earned the trust and respect of the warden and was placed in charge of the other prisoners. One day he noticed that two imprisoned servants of Pharaoh, the butler and the baker, were troubled and tried to help them. Both told him of dreams they'd had which they didn't understand. The Lord enabled him to interpret their dreams, which foretold the execution of the baker, and the pardon and reinstatement of the butler.

"Put in a good word for me!"

"When you return to Pharaoh's house," he said to the butler, "please put in a good word for me. I was kidnapped into Egypt, falsely accused and sent to prison."

Although the butler promised to help, when he was released, he forgot all about Joseph. Two long years went by. Joseph, still jailed, might have languished in prison forever. However, one night Pharaoh had two troubling dreams, and the next morning none of his magicians or wise men could explain their meaning.

Then the butler remembered Joseph! Isn't this an absolutely amazing story? Do you recall what happened next?

Joseph was summoned from prison and came before Pharaoh to hear his dreams. God revealed to Joseph the meaning of the dreams, and he told the interpretation to Pharaoh. There were to be seven years of plenty and bountiful harvest, followed by seven years of terrible drought and famine. To deal with this coming calamity, Joseph recommended storing up part of the harvest during each of the seven bountiful years, then using the surplus during the famine years to keep the nation from dying.

You know what happened—Pharaoh appointed Joseph to be in charge of carrying out that plan, and made him the second most powerful person in the land.

Later, of course, the very brothers who sold Joseph into slavery were forced to come to Egypt and appear before him to buy food for their family in the midst of the famine. When they finally realized who he was, they were terrified.

But Joseph said, *Ye thought evil against me; but God meant it for good...to save much people alive. Now therefore fear ye not: I will nourish you, and your little ones* (Genesis 50:20,21).

What a magnificent adventure life is!

I doubt that any of our journeys through life have had as many side trips and detours as Joseph's. But we certainly can understand that the pathway we follow isn't always straight...or level...or smooth.

At the time, the way we have to go may not even seem pleasant. It is only after we have lived through the struggles and climbed up out of the dark valleys that we can look back and realize that God was leading us every step...and that He has brought us a mighty long way.

Only then can we see that we are living a magnificent adventure...on an incredible journey! Only then can we cry out with the psalmist, *Surely the wrath of man shall praise thee* (Psalm 76:10).

Why is life filled with such uncertainty and stress? Why are we confronted with so many obstacles and challenges along the way? Why did this happen? Why did I have to go through that?

We can never find the answers to these questions and understand life's true meaning if we only look at our circumstances from the *outside*. The answers can be found only as we examine the fabric of our lives from the *inside out!*

A very wise person once said, "In God's economy, nothing is ever lost." This means, first of all, that everything happens for a reason, according to God's plan. Second, every experience of our life is *always* for our good. And third—don't miss this—what happens to us helps equip us to comfort, help, and minister to others down the road!

After God has brought you through a struggle or a trial victoriously, around the bend, you may encounter someone else who is going through that same trial. That's when you can go to them as they experience anxiety and pain, put your arm around them, and say, "I was exactly where you are, and God brought me through to victory. Here's the way to go. Here's what to do. Here's what God wants to do for you!"

Blessed to be a blessing!

I believe that God never blesses us *just for us*…but to equip us to help and bless someone else! *Blessed be God, even the Father of our Lord Jesus Christ, the Father of mercies, and the God of all comfort; who comforteth us in all our tribulation, that we may be able to comfort them which are in any trouble, by the comfort wherewith we ourselves are comforted of God* (2 Corinthians 1:3,4).

This book is intended to encourage you to look at every lesson of life from another point of view—from the perspective the Lord would want you to have…from the *inside out*. Every challenge is for our good—not to cripple us but to make us strong. Every blessing we receive is not just for our enjoyment, but is intended to be a resource we can share with others!

Now our Lord Jesus Christ himself, and God, even our Father, which hath loved us, and hath given us everlasting consolation and good hope through grace, comfort your hearts, and stablish you in every good word and work (2 Thessalonians 2:16,17).

I am sharing my heart with you on these pages in the hope that you, too, will catch the *inside out* vision and become as excited as I about the privilege we have to walk with Him. Take my hand then in Christian fellowship, and let us go on together! You are my brother or my sister in the Lord, and we are traveling with Him on *an incredible journey!*

Chapter One

∞

I DON'T KNOW

As a child I'm told, I asked lots of questions. I used to follow my father around as he worked in his garden, asking him about all kinds of things. I was curious about everything!

"Why do green tomatoes turn red, Daddy? Why do potatoes grow under the ground? Why does corn come inside a wrapper? Why are there so many bugs and worms in the garden? How can they tell what things are good to eat?"

Dad was very patient and never let me know if he got tired of hearing so many "whys." It seemed to me at the time that he always had an answer for any question I could ask. Very, very seldom did he ever say to me, "I really don't know."

I don't know if my dad's ability to always have an answer for me encouraged my inquisitive nature or not. I'm not even certain that his answers were always correct. But to this day I still have a very active sense of curiosity about situations and ideas.

"You ask so many questions!"

My husband and I have traveled all over America and into

fifty other countries of the world on ministry trips. As we encountered strange places and observed unfamiliar customs, I'd have a hundred questions about what things were, why events happened, how long this had been going on, where it started, who was involved, what it all meant — on and on, more and more. Jack sometimes said, "Rexella, you ask so many questions!"

Do you ever wonder about the events and goings on in your world? Like me, do you still find yourself asking a lot of whys and whens?

Today, I often find that people come to me with questions. Although Jack and I weren't privileged to have children to ask the usual million questions about life and the world, we are regularly approached by people who seem to think that because we have spent a lifetime in the ministry, we must have all of the answers. Frequently, we are asked some very difficult questions, the kind for which there really aren't any good, definitive answers. For example, I've been asked why God chose Moses, who stuttered, instead of Aaron, who was artic-ulate, to go before Pharaoh to demand the release of the enslaved Hebrew people. Why did God choose a foreign woman, Ruth of Moab, to be the great-grandmother of David instead of some sweet Jewish girl? Why did Jesus choose a thief and a traitor, Judas, to be one of His twelve disciples? Why did God choose for His beloved Son to be born in a stable instead of a palace?

Why, God, why?

There are also some other questions — the really hard, troubling kind that bring tears to my eyes and leave my heart aching inside. Just in the last several months, desperately hurting people have asked: "Why did my wife (or husband) die just as we were beginning our lives? Why was my child born with an incurable disease? Why didn't my marriage last? Why is life such a struggle for so many good people who have physical ailments or financial reverses? Why do some have so much and others so little? It doesn't seem fair. Why is there never any lasting peace in the Middle East?" Why did 9/11/01 occur?

Time after time, I find myself responding to impossible, imponderable questions like these with a simple, "I don't know." There is no other honest reply I can give.

Not long ago, a friend shared with me a little story that blessed my heart and helped me think more clearly about why certain things happen in our lives. This story is so powerful that it may bring the light of understanding to you or someone you know who is struggling to find any meaning or purpose to life.

Interrupted miracle

According to the story, a man once found the cocoon of a butterfly and decided to watch the miracle of metamorphosis. One day a small opening appeared in the cocoon and the head of the butterfly emerged. The man watched in fascination as it writhed and wriggled, struggling to force its body through the little hole.

To his consternation, the struggle went on for hours until the exhausted butterfly seemed to stop making any progress— it appeared that the creature had gotten as far as it could and was unable to go any further. After a long time, the man couldn't stand it any longer. So, to help the butterfly, he took some small scissors and snipped off the tough wall of the cocoon.

Then the man sat back to watch, fully expecting at any moment to see the butterfly's wings unfold and expand to support the body, which would contract in time. But it didn't happen! In fact, the butterfly spent the rest of its life crawling around with a deformed body and shriveled wings, never able to fly.

What the well-intentioned man did not understand was that the butterfly's struggle to get through the tiny hole in the constricting cocoon was necessary to force fluid from its body into its wings. Only the ongoing, wearisome struggle prepared the butterfly for flight once it achieved its freedom from the cocoon.

Sometimes struggles are exactly what we need if we are to fully develop in our lives. At the time, our trial and ordeal may not make sense or be understandable at all, and certainly does not seem to be part of a loving God's best plan for us. But if He allowed us to go through our lives without challenges or obstacles, the result might be crippling. We would not be as strong as He intended for us to be, and perhaps we could never fly.

Isn't this a dramatic and remarkable story? And what a powerful truth it embodies. When you look back at the hard places in your life — perhaps even the ongoing struggle you are facing right now — realize that God knows who you are and where you are. His plan for your life is good. No matter how trapped you may feel by what seems to be cruel circumstances, God's plan is for you to be free, and to fly!

From Trials to Triumph

One of the most amazing stories in the entire Bible is the account of the life of Joseph. When he shared the dreams God gave him, his father rebuked him and his brothers abused him. Sold into slavery in a strange land, his master's wife deceived him and he was banished to a dungeon. Then, even those he tried to help in prison betrayed and forgot him. Who could ever explain so much misfortune and sorrow?

Yet God used all Joseph's miseries and crushing circumstances to prepare him and put him in position to play a crucial role in history. We all know how God raised him up when the time came for him to be used to save an entire nation in the time of famine, including his own family.

But Joseph never would have developed into one of the most powerful men in all the world if he had not struggled his way through the bondage of the cocoon. What if Joseph had gone down to Egypt and sat around crying, "Woe is me. Why am I so persecuted?" He never would have developed and used the talents God had given to him. And he probably would have sat in jail for the rest of his life.

Joseph was willing to struggle within the cocoon. He was willing to accept what God had done even when he didn't understand it. He remained determined to become better, not bitter. As a result, the day came when Joseph, looking back at all the unanswerable whys of his life, could say to his brothers, *As for you, ye thought evil against me; but God meant it unto good* (Genesis 50:20).

Here's another inspiring thought you may want to keep to encourage you during tough times—

> *I asked for strength.*
> God gave me difficulties to make me strong.
> *I asked for wisdom.*
> God gave me problems to solve.
> *I asked for prosperity.*
> God gave me a brain and brawn to work.
> *I asked for courage.*
> He gave me danger to overcome.
> *I asked for love.*
> God gave me troubled people to help.
> *I asked for favor.*
> He gave me opportunity.
> *I received nothing I wanted.*
> I got everything I needed!

So much truth in so few words! And maybe—just maybe—they help answer some of the whys in your life. For we can never be all that God wants us to be until we've gone through the process of development which often is found only in the struggle. The Word of God helps us to grow as we strain our way out of the cocoon of difficulty. Our trust and faith in the Lord help us to develop the wings we need to take flight.

Instead of saying, "I don't know why this has to be in my life," we can say, "Thank You, God, for helping me develop into what You want me to be." But this attitude can only come when we view ourselves from the *Inside Out*.

It may be that you have spent too much of your life trying to avoid difficulty, running from obstacles, shrinking back from trials. As a result, you may feel that you have ended up like the butterfly in the story, with a swollen body and shriveled wings, never having achieved your potential or God's perfect plan.

Launch out into the deep

Unlike that unfortunate butterfly, it is not too late for you. God has given you the marvelous privilege of being able to choose to change. You have the opportunity once again to launch out into the deep and put your faith in the Lord. You can begin again to grow and develop. There are still challenges to face, battles to fight, races to be won. There are still opportunities to exercise your shriveled wings of faith until a marvelous metamorphosis takes place in your body, soul, and spirit. The day can yet come when you will take flight and be all that He wants you to be.

How can this happen? I don't know how. I only know it *can* happen, and does! But even in the process of not knowing, we can be growing. We don't have to fully understand the secrets of God to benefit from them. His mind is too wonderful for us to completely comprehend.

The Word of God declares, *The secret things belong unto the Lord our God: but those things which are revealed belong unto us and to our children for ever, that we may do all the words of this law* (Deuteronomy 29:29).

Sooner or later, all of us must reach the place where we don't worry and fret about the secret things, the unknown, the unexplainable questions. Standing fast in trust and faith, we can say, "Why ask why?" and be content.

How precious, then, to know that we do not have to walk through the dark days of our lives without the sustaining faith of God. The Apostle Paul reminds us of the glorious truth that *God hath dealt to every man the measure of faith* (Romans 12:3). This is why, even when we can't answer the questions that life throws at us, we still know the Answer!

One of my favorite old gospel songs says it beautifully—

> *Many things about tomorrow*
> *I don't seem to understand,*
> *But I know who holds tomorrow,*
> *And I know who holds my hand.*

Oh, my dear friend, I bless you today in the name of our Lord Jesus Christ. I pray that God will guide your path and make it bright. I pray that He will dispel the darkness around you so your feet will never stumble out of His plan. Expect the desires of your heart to come true and receive Christ's peace as a reality, resting upon everything you do. And may goodness and mercy follow you all the days of your life. Amen, and Amen.

Chapter Two

∞

NOTHING FOR ME

I saw her the moment I stood up to sing. She was in a wheel-chair, sitting toward the front of the crowded auditorium. I could immediately tell that she was tiny and frail, one of the "small" people whose bodies never fully develop. Although she must have been about twenty years of age, she was hardly bigger than a child, with a short upper torso and fragile, doll-like arms.

Immobile from the waist down, with tiny little legs that barely reached the edge of the seat, she obviously had spent her life confined to that wheelchair. But she was radiant, posi-tively beaming with joy. She was entering into the service with all of her heart, enjoying everything that was happening.

The music "intro" cued me to begin my song, and I poured out my heart and testimony to the great crowd assembled there in Chattanooga's Tennessee College Auditorium. Thanks to the anointing of the Holy Spirit, I was able to finish minis-tering my musical message that night. But each time I glanced over at that little face in the wheelchair, beaming with such exuberance, the lump in my throat made it hard for me to get through my song...and my own face was soon wet with tears.

I can see her even now with the eyes of my mind, lifting up her little arms and hands in praise, her face aglow with love and happiness, worshipping God as I sang. I will never, ever forget that night and that extraordinary young woman as long as I live.

Some people who tune in our weekly telecast, "Jack Van Impe Presents," may not know that Jack and I spent many years on the road, conducting crusades. We ministered in some 800 single church meetings across America. Then, much like the incomparable Billy Graham, we conducted 270 mass area-wide crusades in auditoriums, fairgrounds, ballparks, and football stadiums, with crowds of ten to twelve thousand people each night. Over the years, we stood face to face with some 10 million people and registered 600,000 decisions for Christ in these meetings.

In those years, I often played the piano for the services, and almost always I sang just before Jack came to preach. Usually I also spoke sometime during the week for a ladies luncheon or a Christian club meeting.

Each night after the invitation and prayer service, Jack and I stayed behind in the auditorium to talk with people. We signed thousands of Bibles and had our picture taken with babies or sometimes entire families. We had a great time getting acquainted with people and having fellowship with the family of God.

Caring for others

On that particular night, as I was visiting with the Chattanooga area people who had come up after the service to greet me, suddenly there she was—the young woman in the wheelchair. She was still beaming, and seemed so excited to shake my hand. After a couple of moments, she asked, "Rexella, I wonder if you would pray with me about a couple of things?"

"Of course, I'd be happy to," I replied. "What's on your heart?"

She told me that she was attending the Christian classes at Tennessee College and had a couple of roommates who had special needs. She told me about one girl who needed prayer for a family problem, and another who was struggling financially. I could sense her sincere and genuine concern for her friends.

I learned later that this girl, despite her severe disabilities, had enrolled in school because she wanted to serve the Lord in some way. Because of her positive attitude and indomitable spirit, everybody on campus knew and respected her. Her roommates and others helped her get around, lifting her up and down stairs and carrying her books. Everybody loved to be around her, laughing with her and soaking up the love that just poured out of her.

When she finished telling me about her friends' prayer requests, I said, "Honey, is there anything I can pray about for you?"

She flashed her bright smile again and said softly, "Oh, no, Rexella, nothing for me!"

There she sat in her wheelchair, so small and frail, physically helpless, with no hope of ever getting better. Yet she was rich in faith and love, reaching outside of her handicapped world to think of and care for others instead of herself. She viewed her life from the *Inside Out.*

I knelt down and embraced her, tears once again coursing down my cheeks. Her little body was so small and slight inside my arms...but she made a major impact in my heart. Her living example and unspoken testimony has witnessed to me countless times over the years. She shook my prayer life and changed my world. I have never been the same since I met her that night.

Nothing for me!

How many times have I been able to say that in my prayers—and really mean it? Or when I go to God in prayer, is it always for me? Am I always asking just for myself?

Avoid the "me first" mentality

Yes, I realize that we are invited to take our burdens to the

Lord and leave them there. Our heavenly Father wants to give us good things, and He does! Jesus said, *Ask, and ye shall receive* (John 16:24).

But I think that sometimes we can become very self-centered in our prayer lives, thinking only about those things that benefit us. I can't help but believe that perhaps God would smile on us even more if just once in a while, we would come, saying, "Lord, I just want to spend some time with You, worshipping, praising, giving thanks. I just want to embrace You and have fellowship with You. I just want to love You and be in Your presence."

Many people I've talked with about this have said, "I don't remember ever praying without asking God for something...at least one thing for me." One lady said, "Even if I try not to be self-centered when I pray, it seems like I end up saying, 'Lord, bless me today' or 'Lord be with me in this or that.'"

We certainly seem to be living in a "me first" society, don't we? What's in it for me? What can I get? How can I get ahead? Even driving on the streets can be a little scary, with so many drivers racing through traffic lights, cutting off other drivers, doing what's convenient for them. But so many are finding that a "me first" mentality is empty and lonely...and small.

In fact, I once heard that a person wrapped up in himself makes a very small package! Do you know anybody like that?

We can't fill up our lives with things. We can't fill up our lives with ourselves. Life is only full and rich when we fill up our lives with the Lord and others.

Fill up your life with the Lord

Have you tried it? I implore you to spend an entire devotional time with the Lord with a "nothing for me" attitude. In fact, purpose in your heart to ask for nothing. Just praise Him for Who He is. Thank Him for what He has done. Be still and know that He is God...and that you have the privilege of being in His presence. Can you do it? Will you try?

Do you know what will happen? At first you'll be tempted

to start asking. Needs, burdens, and concerns will flood into your mind. But keep turning the focus of your attention away from yourself and back upon Him. Praise Him, thank Him, love Him. Slow yourself down and just rest in His presence.

I believe that as soon as you can genuinely say, "Nothing for me, Lord," He will begin giving you some really precious things just because you aren't asking. What kind of gifts am I talking about?

First, you may realize a new sense of peace. When you tune out life's problems, frustrations, and needs and focus instead on the goodness of God, you open yourself up to Him. He is a God who brings order out of chaos and calms the troubled sea. Jesus said, ...*my peace I give unto you: not as the world giveth, give I unto you. Let not your heart be troubled, neither let it be afraid* (John 14:27). It often happens that when you seek for nothing but God, He provides what you truly need. *But my God shall supply all your need according to His riches in glory by Christ Jesus* (Philippians 4:19).

Second, you will find that your confidence is renewed when you spend time in God's presence. Have you ever noticed how sure and secure little children are when they are with their moms or dads? Doubt and fear are not a problem. Notice, too, that confidence is not something you normally ask for—it comes naturally in His presence, dispelling uncertainty and confusion. The Word of God says, *For the Lord shall be thy confidence...* (Proverbs 3:26).

And third, spending time with God will do wonders for your joy! There is little joy in selfishness and self-centeredness. The psalmist cried out to God, ...*in thy presence is fullness of joy...* (Psalm 16:11). Joy is crucial to our well-being, and creates the proper atmosphere for the cultivation of other essential qualities of victorious living.

Do you have a joy shortage?

For example, do you sometimes feel weak and defeated? You may have a joy shortage. Why do I say that? Because the

Word of God says ...*the joy of the Lord is your strength* (Nehemiah 8:10).

I have a little acrostic written in my Bible which may be familiar to you. It is **J-O-Y**

Jesus first, **O**thers next, **Y**ourself last! And you know, putting this truth into practice really works!

Somehow it reminds me of the beautiful young woman in the wheelchair I met that night in Chattanooga. The joy of the Lord was all over her, radiating out from her like a light. The minute I stood up, my eyes were drawn to her. Throughout the service, I noticed that she was worshipping Jesus. Then afterward, when she came to me, her concern was for others, asking me to pray for the needs of her friends. And she certainly put herself last. Even when I asked if I could pray for her, she quickly replied, "Nothing for me."

Oh, if only we could be as thoughtful in approaching God as we are in fulfilling social obligations. When we receive a gift from a friend, we write a thank you note. We wouldn't think of adding a postscript and asking for something else!

How much we have to thank the Lord for. Every day we should give thanks for the very life that we have, the breath that we breathe, the good health we enjoy, the blessings of home, clothes, food, and rest. Why do we fail to remember all that we have to be thankful for?

Over the years, my husband and I have traveled in scores of countries around the world. In so many of these places, the people live in poverty and great need, or under oppressive political regimes. Sometimes I have wondered why I have been so blessed to live in America where even our poorest citizens have more than most people in the rest of the world. Yet too often we seem to take it for granted and fail to give thanks from a grateful heart.

On our international telecast, we invite people to contact us via the Internet. Hundreds of thousands do. In fact, not long ago we had about a million individual visits to our websight in a single month, with contacts from 112 countries. And you'd be amazed at how many of these dear people expressed gratitude for our sharing the gospel with them.

Recently Jack and I received an email from a member of Parliament in the Ukraine, one of the former Soviet Republics. He wrote to thank us for sending our telecast via satellite into his country to minister the Gospel to his people. I felt so humble to read that beautiful letter. I almost felt that I should be the one saying thanks for allowing us to share the Gospel and through it, obey Christ's Great Commission.

How can I say thanks?

Andre Crouch's beautiful song, "My Tribute," begins with the words, "How can I say thanks...?" I have had that exact same feeling in my heart so many times. When I bow before the Lord and try to express my gratitude, so often I have cried out, "Oh God, how can I ever thank You for all You have given, for all You have done for me? What could I possibly do for you?"

I found the answer in the words of Jesus — *Verily I say unto you, Inasmuch as ye have done it unto one of the least of these my brethren, ye have done it unto me* (Matthew 25:40).

Look around you and find the people that no one else is helping. Find those who are needy, sick, and alone, the weak and helpless, the lost and dying. Reach out to them in love and compassion. Point them to the Savior and Healer. Lift up Jesus. As you minister to them you will minister to Him!

I promise that as you do this, your life will become exciting and wonderful. Love will light your pathway. The presence of the Lord will be so near that you will never walk alone.

When you reach that place, one day someone will ask what personal need or request you'd like him to pray with you about. And you'll just smile and shake your head and say—

"Nothing for me!"

Chapter Three

I'M TIRED

So much happens so quickly during any given year. Just think about the last twelve months and you will remember saying, "Lord, I'm so tired-I'm just worn out!" Have you ever felt that way?

Exhaustion can be a dangerous condition, making us vulnerable to discouragement and attacks from the devil, the enemy of our soul. Fatigue seems to amplify the concerns of life, whether they be health problems, financial pressure, or spiritual concerns for ourselves or loved ones.

Often when we're really worn out, anxieties and indecision can paralyze our mind and steal away our peace, keeping us awake and troubled into the midnight hours. So we get even more tired, and our problems seem even bigger and our load that much heavier.

Does any of this sound familiar? Then you've come to the right place! There is hope and help for you, and a place you can go for rest and renewal.

"Lord, I Need a Nap"

One of my fondest memories from the years Jack and I spent on the road in citywide crusades happened on the closing night of a meeting in Rochester, New York. As was our custom, after the service, we were down front greeting people, signing Bibles, and enjoying fellowship with old and new friends. I was especially enjoying the children who gathered around us.

One little guy was so cute that I couldn't resist reaching down and picking him up. He smiled at me, then nestled into my arms and murmured, "I'm tired ... I need a nap." Then he put his little head on my shoulder and started to go to sleep. It was so sweet. When his dad came to take him from me a few minutes later, I was sorry to see him go.

What a beautiful example of what we can — and should — do when we're weary. With childlike faith and trust, we should go into the presence of our heavenly Father and find rest in God. We should just climb up into His arms and say, "Lord, I'm tired — I need a nap."

That's exactly what the Lord wants us to do. He has already extended the invitation — *Come unto me, all ye that labour and are heavy laden, and I will give you rest* (Matthew 11:28). Are you worn out and burdened down? Come to Jesus and find rest! The apostle Peter also advises us to go to the Lord — *Casting all your care on him; for he careth for you* (1 Peter 5:7).

What a marvelous privilege is ours. But have you ever noticed that sometimes we try to muddle along on our own, attempting to get by in our own strength? Or even if we go to the Lord, somehow it's difficult to completely leave our burdens with Him.

A beautiful, old gospel song says, "Take your burdens to the Lord and leave them there." Over the years, I've learned to go to the Lord when I'm tired and weary, but sometimes I still have a hard time *leaving* my burdens and cares at the cross. It's so easy to get up from my place of prayer and communion with God and pick up my heavy load again! Do you know what

I mean?

Jack and I receive many beautiful letters from friends who see our television program and are blessed. Here's one that says, "I want to thank you both for helping my spirit stay up when it seems like I can't go on another day."

I'm glad we can offer encouragement, but how much better if this friend could learn to find rest and help in God every day. There are multitudes of people — unbelievers and believers alike — who somehow cannot find peace in a troubled world. They have not learned the beauty of trust. Instead of giving their worries to God, they keep trying to carry them on their own.

Learning to Trust

I'll never forget when I learned the meaning of trust. I've used this illustration before but it bears repeating. When my brothers and I were quite young, my mother and dad would take us swimming in a beautiful, freshwater stream that had a nice little natural waterfall. My elder brother would go to the top of the waterfall and jump down into a pool of water below. It looked like great fun!

The first time I went to the top of the waterfall, I was very hesitant to jump. My father was down below, and he called out, "Jump, Rexella. Jump and I'll catch you!"

It seemed such a long way down, and the waterfall was splashing and foaming. I wanted to back away, but I could see my father reaching up to me. I knew I could trust him completely. So finally, heart pounding and body shivering in apprehension, I jumped! I plunged into the turbulence of the waterfall, down under the surface of the natural pool below. As I came up, half laughing, half crying, almost ready to panic — Dad's strong arms grabbed me and lifted me up! After that, I was ready to try it again and again.

My trust in my father made all the difference. His calm assurance inspired confidence in me, and I overcame my fear.

How much more is our heavenly Father able to care for us

and meet our needs? No matter what your situation may be today, Christ is your answer. You can go to Him and say, "Lord, I'm trusting You today to help me. I'm exhausted from carrying my burdens. I'm physically tired from the rush of the season. Now I'm coming into a new year, and I want to recommit my life, my direction, and my path to You."

When you open your heart to God, He will come in and fill you with His peace, mercy, and strength. I can guarantee you that He will lift you up and keep you from falling. God says, *As one whom his mother comforteth, so will I comfort you; and ye shall be comforted* ... (Isaiah 66:13). Isn't that a beautiful promise?

The Comforter in You

When you are rested, strengthened, and comforted by the power of God, you can reach out to help and minister to others. The Word of God says that He ... *comforteth us in all our tribulation, that we may be able to comfort them which are in any trouble, by the comfort wherewith we ourselves are comforted of God* (2 Corinthians 1:4).

The Bible teaches us to help others. For example, Galatians 6:2 says, *Bear ye one another's burdens, and so fulfil the law of Christ.* And there are many biblical examples of this.

When the Old Testament character, Job, went through his ordeal, his friends came to his side ... *for they had made an appointment together to come to mourn with him and to comfort him* (Job 2:11). And when Lazarus died, we're told that *many of the Jews came to Martha and Mary, to comfort them concerning their brother* (John 11:19).

I believe we should be there for our friends and do all that is in our power to help. We can stand with them in persecution and tribulation. We can help to sustain them in times of trouble. But there are limits to what we are able to do. Too often we are unable to change circumstances. Only God can change any situation and meet every need.

Perhaps the best way we can help is to point our friends to

the Lord and comfort them with the promises of His Word. What we have to say in the time of trouble might mean very little, but what God has to say means everything.

The apostle Paul wrote in Philippians 4:6-7, *Be careful for nothing: but in everything by prayer and supplication with thanksgiving let your requests be make known unto God. And the peace of God, which passeth all understanding, shall keep your hearts and minds through Christ Jesus.* Truly, the Apostle Paul viewed life from the *Inside Out.*

I believe we tire more quickly when we are struggling alone than when someone is with us, don't you? The writer of Ecclesiastes observed that *two are better than one; because they have a good reward for their labour* (4:9).

Thank God, we never have to be alone! Even when no human friend is near to us, we have the promise of Jesus himself—*Lo, I am with you always, even unto the end of the age* (Matthew 28:20). Sometimes we may not be aware of the presence of God, but He is with us all the time. We need to learn to practice His presence and acknowledge Him. The minute we speak to the Holy Spirit, He makes us aware that He is not only with us, but in us as well (1 Corinthians 3:16).

When He draws near, we immediately sense the warmth of His love. Have you noticed how difficult it is to rest when you are cold? I can't go to sleep when I am shivering. But when I am secure and warm in the arms of my husband, I can relax and go right to sleep.

This is what happens to us when we are enveloped in the warmth of God's love. Only then can we say, "God, I'm so tired that I must take a little nap and let You work on my problems. Here, I give them to You so I can rest."

Worry: The Fruit of a Divided Mind

In reading the hundreds and hundreds of letter and e-mails Jack and I get each week, we've noticed how many people talk about being so tired and exhausted, and how they feel overwhelmed by life and feel unable to cope with all the challenges they face.

This seems to go along with recent medical studies confirming that a large percentage of Americans don't get enough rest. They don't sleep enough, and they don't sleep well. So they wake up groggy and still tired.

At the same time, most people try to cram so much activity into their lives that they keep themselves exhausted. So they push themselves to the limit, until that can't go anymore. Then they worry about that!

The Greek word for worry, I'm told, actually refers to a divided mind. When our mind is divided and in a state of unrest, we can't rest and sleep. So the problem keeps getting worse. James 1:8 states: *A double minded man is unstable in all his ways.*

Worn out, exhausted, and sapped by fatigue, people's natural immunity and resistance gets low, and they are vulnerable to germs, viruses, and disease. Or they get so tired that they become fearful and disheartened by the ongoing challenges of modern life. And the downward spiral continues.

But there is a better way. Don't allow yourself to be dragged down by the weariness of the world. Find rest and peace by walking daily in the presence of God. Discover with Paul, that *... He is not far from every one of us: for in Him we live, and move, and have our being...* (Acts 17:27, 28).

Hear and heed the invitation of our Lord and Savior who said to: *Come unto me, all ye that labour and are heavy laden, and I will give you rest. Take my yoke upon you, and learn of me; for I am meek and lowly in heart: and ye shall find rest unto your souls. For my yoke is easy, and my burden is light* (Matthew 11:28-30).

Begin today with a new trust in the Lord. May this be your prayer, "Lord, I'm tired of being tired. Help me to trust You to take all my burdens and give me Your rest. Amen."

Chapter Four

◯◯

THE SILENT FORCE OF FAITH, HOPE AND LOVE

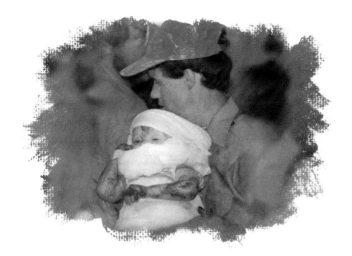

A nd now abideth faith, hope, charity [love], *these three; but the greatest of these is charity* [love] (1 Corinthians 13:13).

There are unseen forces in the world that are vitally important in the course of human events. These forces shape individual lives and even influence world affairs.

Recognizing that these forces exist can be intimidating. For some people, the idea that they might not be in control of what happens in their lives can actually be emotionally crippling. As Christians, we need never feel intimidated by anything. As the old gospel song suggests, we may not know what tomorrow holds, but we know who holds our tomorrows. Ultimately, God is in control of all things to come.

We do have the power to make many life-controlling decisions. Every individual has the opportunity to perpetuate good or evil...to uplift Christ or approve the works of Satan... to show love or hate, joy or sorrow.

When faced with the fateful forces of life, we have an arsenal of divine forces at our disposal that can help us withstand any storm and overcome any adversity. Faith. Hope. Love.

Too often these forces are just words to us and we fail to fully understand the explosive power that is ours. God, in His unchanging Word, gives unprecedented value to these truths. They are the keys to unlimited power and spiritual wealth in your life and mine.

The baby who fell in the well

Some time ago our attention was focused on a tiny little child in Midland, Texas, who had fallen into an abandoned oil well. Only 18 months old, plucky little Jessica McClure captured the heart of the whole nation. Students, business people, workers, housewives, even the First Lady — we all showed our interest and concern for her plight. People across the country prayed, sent cards and letters, offered assistance, telephoned — whatever they could do. And the people in the Texas communities nearby dropped what they were doing and went to help. They labored without being asked…not asking for pay… around the clock until the ordeal was over.

I was so impressed with the actions of Jessica's family and close friends. I'll never forget seeing the TV news pictures of them standing in a circle, holding hands, praying for God's help. The strength of their faith was transmitted nation wide. It never wavered!

We all can have this kind of faith, which Hebrews 11 defines as *the substance of things hoped for, the evidence of things not seen.* I believe faith is an inner stability produced by the Holy Spirit that enables us to trust. And it is trust that dispels doubt, fear, and uncertainty.

How wonderful to know we have a counter-force that can work in our behalf when we're faced with those unseen, uncontrollable forces and circumstances of life. The force of faith will help us trust God for peace and victory — even in the face of seemingly insurmountable obstacles like Jessica McClure and her family faced.

The force of faith

The silent force of faith is indescribably powerful. With faith a shepherd boy takes five stones and a slingshot and defeats Goliath, the military champion. With faith, Moses stretches out a wooden stick over the Red Sea and the waters roll back to provide a path of safety for God's people.

You may well be facing conflicts, disasters, heartaches, and darkness as deep as a well. But as you rely on the unseen force of faith, trust will rise up inside you and sustain you until deliverance comes — for the Lord *will* bring you through.

Most Important of all, the force of faith even overcomes the fatal curse of sin and helps us receive Christ's salvation and everlasting life. *For by grace are ye saved through faith* (Ephesians 2:8).

The force of hope

The second silent force you can use is hope. What a devastating thing to feel utterly hopeless — to believe there is no remedy for your desperate situation!

Without hope, life cannot long endure. With hope — even the tiniest spark — we can keep holding on, keep waiting and watching until victory comes.

Just as faith produces trust, hope produces joy and peace. Surely it was the hope and peace of that precious little girl in the Texas well that helped save her life.

Can you imagine her cries of fear and distress? "Mommy, I'm hurt, I can't move. It's so dark and I'm afraid. I'm cold. I'm hungry. Please help me!" And she listened for a voice at the top of the well —her mother's. That voice so filled her with hope and encouragement, I'm told little Jessica cried very little. She had peace — even joy. Down in her dark, cold trap, she could even sing!

Oh, my friend, here's a truth that is absolutely overwhelming. You and I can have hope in the wells of life. Down in our prisons of darkness and pain, we can hear a Voice from above — the voice of our Father saying, "Fear not! *Lo, I am with you alway, even unto the end of the world* (Matthew 28:20).

There is hope! And there is joy and peace for you today. Are you trapped by emotional needs? Hear the voice of the Lord saying, *Come unto me, all ye that labour and are heavy laden, and I will give you rest* (Matthew 11:28).

Are you so buried by financial and material needs that it seems you'll never again see the light of day? Listen! God's promise is sufficient for you. *My God shall supply all your need according to his riches in glory by Christ Jesus* (Philippians 4:19). Are you worried, troubled, depressed? Oh, hear the voice of hope — *Casting all your care upon him; for he careth for you* (1 Peter 5:7).

I tell you, there is no hole so deep that hope cannot reach. And no place so low that God cannot lift you out. Use the silent force of hope God has given you... and let joy and peace change your world.

Remember, Jesus has experienced every emotional temptation or physical pain that we could ever experience. He was *in all points tempted like as we are, yet without sin* (Hebrews 4:15). Jesus was not tempted to see if He *would* sin, but to show that He *could not* sin, for He is God.

He understands your need. He is greater than your need... and He cares about your need. So you can have hope.

The force of love

The third and greatest unseen force you have at your disposal is love. Love is so powerful — and so misunderstood. Faith produces trust. Hope produces joy and peace. But love produces manifold blessings.

The newspaper headlines reporting the drama in Midland, Texas, said: "USA Opens Its Heart to Jessica:" Why? I believe one reason people loved this child so much was that they saw faith in her family and hope in her — qualities America needs so desperately today. Especially since the tragedy of 9/11/01. And remember how their love was expressed —in action. That's because love, being the essence of God's divine nature, is not just a noun — it's a verb, it is action. So in loving Jessica, people helped, worked, gave… they poured themselves out. And they didn't stop loving until she was rescued and brought out of that well, alive and safe. In a thrilling, exciting way, they started *living* the Bible and producing the manifold fruits of love described in 1 Corinthians 13:4-8.

I know you've read these familiar scriptures many times, but let's think about them in terms we can understand without question. The silent force of love that God pours through us is absolutely beautiful.

This love produces an uncomplaining spirit that cares for others. It is not jealous, pushy, conceited, or ill-mannered. This love does not try to advance itself, does not pout or become hurt easily. It does not think the worst of others, and is not happy when someone falls into sin but is happy to hear good things about him. Love bears all things and helps others with their burdens. Love endures… and refuses discouragement.

Do you have that kind of love? Oh, it's important to have faith. It's important to have hope. But God's Word declares that the greatest force of all is love.

I urge you to examine yourself from the *Inside Out* to be sure you have the silent force of faith, hope, and love —especially love — within. The only way to have it is to go to the One who gives this perfect gift — Jesus Christ.

I challenge you to join Jack and me in trusting, rejoicing, hoping, and loving in Christ. Using this silent force together, we can change ourselves . . . and make such an impact on our world for Christ that it will never again be the same.

Chapter Five

AND THEN THE SPARROW CAME

Every morning, I take food out into our back yard to feed the squirrels and birds. Michigan winters can be very cold, and wild creatures have a difficult time finding food when the ground is covered by snow. So one of the simple joys of my life is putting out bread or peanuts, sometimes seeds or nuts, for them.

The squirrels are real clowns, cavorting and chattering at each other as they scamper all around the yard and into the shrubs and trees. Most mornings they are joined by all kinds of birds, small and large. Jack and I sit at the breakfast table and enjoy our own private kaleidoscope of color and motion just outside the windows of our cozy kitchen as we enjoy a second cup of coffee.

Feeding the squirrels was the way I discovered our second cat, Bon Bon, a long-haired white outdoor cat. He had been living in a wooded area near our home, and came to snatch some of the food I put out each morning for the squirrels. He was malnourished, emaciated and very wary of people.

I've already related in a previous article the story of how I began putting food out for this cat, then talking to him and trying to win his confidence. After a while, he even let Jack and me touch him, and gradually we were able to make friends and nurse Bon Bon back to total, thriving, glorious health.

That was almost four and one half years ago, and you would be amazed at the change that took place. He was magnificently beautiful, a virtual show cat, with long, flowing fur, shining yellow eyes, and a loving disposition. Bon Bon was happy, trusting, and caring. He would come into the kitchen every morning to look around, and loved to have either Jack or me stroke his fur while he ate. Our other cat, Fenica, would tolerate him as long as he never forgot that she is mistress of the house!

So after his morning visit, Bon Bon was always ready to go back outside. He had a comfortable little doo-loo in the yard in which to sleep, because he refused to stay in the house overnight, and there, sheltered from the wind, he would watch the same squirrels from which he used to steal food. From time to time he still liked to leave the yard and patrol the neighborhood, but he was never gone too long.

But then, as we shared on our television program, while driving home one evening we found Bon Bon in the road after being hit by a car. Our hearts were deeply saddened, but the cards and notes that many of our viewers sent, touched Jack and me deeply and comforted us more than I can say.

A lesson from our feathered friends

But today I'm really not writing about either cats or squirrels, but birds. Just in the past few weeks, Jack and I have enjoyed watching an abundance of our feathered friends just outside our window. We've seen the scarlet splendor of several cardinals, the showy red-breasted robins, and the raucous but gorgeous bluejays. There are often blackbirds swarming the trees and bushes in our yard, and from time to time we've seen tiny, little canary-yellow birds, perhaps finches of some kind. Each bird is different—some quiet, some shrill, some timid and some bold. They differ in sizes and colors—but each so beautiful in its own way.

The other morning after Jack had already gone up to his office, I got another cup of coffee and sat down again. I just felt like thanking the Lord for the simple wonders of His creation that bless me so much each morning. As I mused, the food I'd scattered for the birds was pretty well picked over and most of the birds flitted away.

And then the sparrow came. I noticed a blur of motion out of the corner of my eye, then saw a small, grayish-brown bird quietly looking for crumbs left behind by the others. Unobtrusive and inconspicuous, the sparrow hopped around looking for a little crust here, a bite there. Of course, after a few moments, I couldn't resist tossing out a few more scraps of leftover toast.

But as I cleaned up the breakfast dishes so I could get ready for the rest of my day, I couldn't get that little sparrow off my mind. And I began to think about some people I'd observed over the years who were a bit like that little gray bird. They seemed to go through life unnoticed, unappreciated, living on leftovers, with no voice in what was going on around them.

Yet Jesus specifically mentioned the sparrow as an example of something the world might disdain, but God values. He declared that not one of them fell to the ground without His notice, and added, *Fear ye not therefore, ye are of more value than many sparrows* (see Matthew 10:29, 31).

Isn't it interesting that the Lord didn't mention the swan or peacock, the eagle, or even the songbird as attracting God's attention, but the lowly sparrow. Why, then, does it seem that men so often are attracted and influenced by the beautiful and well-groomed people of the world, giving honor and position to the wealthy and powerful instead of the poor and humble?

The Apostle James warned against such respect of

persons. He wrote, *For if there come unto your assembly a man with a gold ring, in goodly apparel, and there come in also a poor man in vile raiment; and ye have respect to him that weareth the gay* (or expensive) *clothing, and say unto him, Sit thou here in a good place; and say to the poor, Stand thou there, or sit here under my footstool: are ye not then partial in yourselves, and are become judges of evil thoughts?* (James 2:2-4).

The Bible is very clear that *God is no respecter of persons* (Acts 10:34).

The Lord looks at the heart

Why does the Bible make such a point of challenging our value system? Because man has a tendency to be unduly attracted and influenced by the senses, by the sight, sound, smell, and touch gates rather than the heart gate. In fact, the Bible says, *...the Lord seeth not as man seeth; for man looketh on the outward appearance, but God looketh on the heart* (1 Samuel 16:7).

At Christmastime when I was opening my presents, I found myself being influenced by the wrappings, reaching for the most attractive package to open first! And while I appreciated all my gifts, I couldn't help noticing that the most beautifully wrapped package didn't always have the most valuable or worthwhile item inside!

Jack and I have been privileged to meet a great many outstanding men and women in ministry. Over the years we have noticed that sometimes a handsome, articulate, polished individual would be given precedence over a less flashy, quieter minister. However, later, when the "sparrow" speaker got his turn, it was obvious to everybody that while he did not have the flashy show of the peacock, the breath-taking music of the songbird, or the bold bravado of the eagle, his words and spirit flowed straight from the heart of God.

I believe you'll find it true that often the showy, flashy things of life are not especially functional. For example, the hood ornament on an automobile may fall off, the shiny paint may get scratched, or the fenders and doors may get a few dings and dents, but that car will keep right on going. If it breaks down, the mechanic will not check the dashboard trim or the leather seats—he will look for mechanical things underneath, hidden from view, that no one ever notices or thinks of until it stops working.

This is why we need to take notice of the people around us who may not be as beautiful and polished as others. We need to love them, pay attention to them, listen to them, allow them to share their thoughts, and make them feel wanted.

When Jesus came to the world, He did not choose to be born into a wealthy family. His first night on earth was spent in a manger bed in a stable, surrounded by barnyard animals and shepherds. During His earthly ministry, Jesus did not spend His time in palaces or with the haughty religious leaders of the day. Rather, He surrounded himself with the poor and needy, the sick and sinful, the common people with needs, hurts, and troubles. He opened His arms to them in compassion and love.

Aren't you glad that presently Jesus doesn't respond just to the rich and powerful or the strong and talented? Even if you feel unloved and unwanted, the Lord knows your name and sees you wherever you are. Never think that your prayers are not heard. No matter how weak your faith or how feeble your call, Jesus will always hear you and lift you up. And no one is too lowly to have value and importance in the eyes of God. Don't misunderstand me—I'm not saying that we should not dress our best or enjoy the blessings and good things we are able to obtain in life. I believe in seeking for knowledge and truth, and getting the best education we can. We do not honor God by being impoverished or slouchy and unkempt because (and please remember this) while God looks on the heart, man still looks on the outward appearance and evaluates the person accordingly. First impressions linger in one's mind.

Look at the world through God's eyes

How can we be effective in serving God and helping to

carry out the Great Commission if we live lives of defeat and want? God has promised to supply our needs, providing all the "things" necessary for living when we seek first His kingdom (see Matthew 6:32). The important thing is that our hearts are right and true and that we view the world through the eyes of Christ rather than the eyes of humanistic values. We must serve Him with the right motives.

If God has blessed you with material things, don't be ashamed of what you have…but don't place too much importance on them. Just find a way to use your possessions for His glory.

If He has given you physical beauty and talent as an artist, singer, orator, or whatever—wonderful! Use what you have to glorify God, and bless other people with your gifts. But be willing to do whatever needs to be done to advance the cause of Christ. The Apostle Paul warns us not to think more highly of ourselves than we ought to (see Romans 12:3).

The Gospel of Mark relates how some of the disciples who followed Jesus got caught up in pride and began jostling for position, asking who would be the greatest in the kingdom (9:34). Two brothers wondered if they would share a position of honor with Jesus, one on His right hand, the other on His left (10:37).

Yet on the night when Jesus was betrayed, as He and His disciples gathered for the Last Supper, none of them was prepared to assume the servant's role. So Jesus got a basin of water and a towel and washed His disciples feet. By His action, the Lord stressed the importance of even the most humble task. There are no unimportant jobs in the kingdom of God!

During the years that Jack and I criss-crossed America and the world in church, auditorium, and stadium crusades, we learned to do whatever had to be done. We unloaded the van, set up the auditorium, gave directions to volunteer ushers and personal workers, rehearsed music, and tended to "a thousand and one" other details. Then we dashed to take a shower and get dressed…often getting back to the auditorium just in time to start the service.

People arriving for the meeting saw us walk in fresh and

clean and probably thought we'd just been resting. After the meeting was over—when we were finished ministering through singing, preaching, praying, and spending time with the people—we'd pack up everything and load it back in the van. Then we'd drive for hours to the next meeting and do it all over again.

"Sparrow" work or spotlight—it's all important

I'm not complaining one bit! I'd do it all over again. But I can tell you there was a lot more "sparrow" work—unseen, behind-the-scenes, unappreciated labor—than there was time spent on stage, in the spotlight.

Now Jack and I spend most of our time producing an international television outreach. People who see us on the "fastest half-hour on TV" can't imagine the hours of research, study, prayer, and preparation that is required for each program. We pray every single day for God's anointing and help. I can't tell you the depth of the humility we feel as we sit down in front of that camera each week, knowing that millions of precious souls will be watching our every move, listening to every word Jack and I say.

Being called to do God's work is a tremendously humbling thing, but it presents an incredible opportunity to give the truth of God's Word to so many hungry hearts each week.

Recently I was having lunch with a friend at a nice restaurant. Three gentlemen walked over to our table, and one of them said, "I'm Judge Smith, and I just wanted you to know how much my family enjoys your weekly telecast. Then he introduced the other men, one of whom was a doctor, who said, "I just won't miss your program—it's such a blessing."

When they left, my friend asked, "Rexella, how does that make you feel?"

I replied, "Knowing that we are reaching into the areas of law and medicine through people like that really touches my heart."

A moment later, a busboy who was clearing the table next

to ours, came over and said, "Is that you, Rexella? Oh, you don't know how much your TV program is helping me. I'm learning so much about the Bible and how to live for God. Excuse me for interrupting, but I just had to say thanks."

He walked away, and again my friend asked how that comment made me feel. I said, "What a privilege to be able to help shape a young person's life in the ways of the Lord. That means just as much as ministering to the judge and the doctor." And it does.

What a joy to be chosen to work with and for our Lord. He has called me. He has called you. Whatever we do has great value in the eyes of God. Are you doing all you can do for the cause of Christ? Together we can serve Him by reaching out in love to others who need Him.

Chapter Six

JUST A CUP OF COFFEE, PLEASE

The news media often calls attention to the large number of homeless and hungry people in our nation's big cities. The scenes of people sleeping on benches, huddling in cardboard boxes, or looking through garbage cans for food are pitiful and troubling. While many of these individuals have ended up on the street through misfortunes beyond their control, even sadder are the cases who are there largely by choice.

As I prayed and thought about this problem, it occurred to me that while not homeless and destitute, most of us, in a spiritual sense, have gotten by with just a cup of coffee and a morsel of bread when we could have been feasting on God's plentiful banquet of spiritual manna. As the Apostle James observes, *Ye have not, because ye ask not* (James 4:2).

My husband, Jack, and I have a favorite little "home cookin'" cafe we often visit when it's just the two of us. It's not fancy at all, but it's a cozy, comfortable place where we can relax—and the food is good. We go there often enough that we know most of the waitresses and many of the regular customers.

For weeks we noticed that a certain man was almost always in the cafe, sitting at the counter. He looked as if he might be homeless, usually dressed in worn, slightly shabby clothes which probably hadn't been laundered in weeks. He was always alone—never did we see him with a friend or ever having a conversation with others at the counter. His countenance was drawn and sad, and one could sense that he had known much sorrow in his lifetime. The waitresses told us he ate only once a day—the rest of the time he just drank coffee "...buy one cup and the refills are free."

Jack and I felt terribly sorry for this man. One night as we were having a light dinner, we looked over at him sitting alone at the counter, nursing his coffee cup, and it made us sad. My hubby called a waitress over and said, "Give that man the best dinner in the house and bring me the bill. Let him pick out anything on the menu and tell him a friend has picked up the tab." "No, Dr. Van Impe, you don't need to do that," said the waitress.

"But I want to," he answered. "He looks like he needs a good meal, and I'd just like to help him a little."

"You don't understand," she said. "That is Mr. _____" (and she named a very well-known and wealthy local family). "His father owned much of the land that is now the City of Troy—he's the heir to millions!"

"But he looks so underprivileged!" I exclaimed.

"Yes, I know," said the waitress, "but he's really a multi-millionaire. He lives like a pauper by choice."

I haven't seen that poor, sad man lately, but recently I've been thinking about his situation. Could it be that many Christians are living like spiritual paupers when they could be enjoying God's manifest blessings every day of their lives? Are they settling for just a cup of coffee when they could be feasting at the Lord's banquet table?

As we face the future, are we anxious about what lies ahead? Will it be a time of happiness and blessing...or endless loneliness and deprivation?

Change your wardrobe

The old man in the cafe was dressed in worn, shabby clothes. Yet he could have been wearing the finest suit from the best tailor in town.

What are you wearing? The Prophet Isaiah said, *I will greatly rejoice in the Lord, my soul shall be joyful in my God, for he hath clothed me with the garments of salvation, he hath covered me with the robe of righteousness, as a bridegroom decketh himself with ornaments, and as a bride adorneth herself with her jewels* (Isaiah 61:10).

Clothe yourself in the wardrobe God has provided for you. Get dressed in His righteousness and see what a change His garments will make in your whole outlook on life. You'll discover a new awareness of God as your Sustainer and Protector. You'll stand taller and walk in trust and confidence.

So resolve to stop dressing like the world and get clothed in His righteousness.

Put sadness aside

The old man in the cafe looked so sad, as if the weight of the world was on his shoulders. Yes, from a worldly perspective, he had everything. He was from a prominent family, with every possible financial advantage at his disposal. If money could buy happiness, he could have had it all.

Christianity is the most joyful of all the world's religions. Yet we often manage to make it appear the most sad and mournful by our actions and our countenance. Mark Twain once had his famous character, Huck Finn, wondering if the mule in the barn had "got religion" because of its long face!

The psalmist exults, *Thou hast put gladness in my heart. For he satisfieth the longing soul, and filleth the hungry soul with goodness* (Psalm 4:7; 107:9).

I think we sometimes develop a bad habit of letting our faces reflect the care and confusion of the world around us instead of the joy and peace of the Lord welling up within us.

If we have full access to God's goodness, gladness, and blessedness, shouldn't our faces show it?

As Christians, our future is as bright as the promises of God. And the Word of God is filled with wonderful promises. Some of my favorites include Christ's promise: *Lo, I am with you alway, even unto the end of the world* (Matthew 28:20) and also God's assurance that *as thy days, so shall thy strength be* (Deuteronomy 33:25).

If we believe God, we have something to smile about.

Be a friend

In all the times we observed the old man in the cafe, Jack and I never saw him with a friend…or ever being friendly with those around him. While others had pleasant conversations and shared personal things with each other, the old man sat alone, without a friend. How sad.

But while true friendship is measured by more than "hellos" and conversations, some people have no friends because they will let no one get close to them.

As the writer of Proverbs observes, *A man that hath friends must show himself friendly: and there is a friend that sticketh closer than a brother* (Proverbs 18:24).

One must be a friend to others to have friends who will share fellowship and companionship in return. And this is an important part of life. But even if earthly friends do fail in times of trouble, we can be secure in knowing that we can have a friend who will stick closer than a brother, in good times and bad.

We know we can count on Him because He has said, *I will never leave thee, nor forsake thee* (Hebrews *13:5*).

When we have such a Friend, why don't we rely on Him more? In the words of the grand old gospel song, "What a Friend We Have in Jesus,"

Oh, what peace we often forfeit,
Oh, what needless pain we bear,

All because we do not carry
Everything to God in prayer.

Eat heartily

I don't think I'll ever forget the old man in the cafe, scrimping by on one meal a day, when he could have had anything on the menu, anytime he wanted it. Yet he'd order "Just a cup of coffee, please" and ask for free refills. How tragic to see a multimillionaire going hungry.

But how much more tragic to have the riches of heaven at our disposal and go through life starving ourselves spiritually! Do you have a Bible? Are you feasting daily on the abundant nourishment found there...or do you hurriedly pull out a single scripture card and glance at it before you dash out into the day?

Compare your biblical diet with Jeremiah's. He said, *Thy words were found, and I did eat them; and thy word was unto me the joy and rejoicing of mine heart: for I am called by thy name, O Lord God of hosts* (Jeremiah 15:16).

Don't settle for just a cup of coffee—eat heartily—even as the Apostle Peter admonished us to do in 1 Peter 2:2, stating: *As newborn babes, desire the sincere milk of the word, that ye may grow thereby.* The psalmist concurs, saying, *O taste and see that the Lord is good: blessed is the man that trusteth in him* (Psalm 34:8).

I heard the story of a man whose dream was to go to America. For years he saved his money to buy passage on a ship. Finally he had just enough, with only a small amount left over.

He took part of the little money he had left and bought some bread and cheese he could take on board. By careful rationing, he thought there would be just enough to last through the voyage.

So he set sail, glad to finally be going to the "promised land." Other passengers were festive and happy, going into the ship's dining room to eat wonderful meals, and strolling about the decks, laughing and having refreshments together.

The man would go to his little cabin at mealtime and eat stale bread and hard cheese.

But he had miscalculated the length of the voyage, and a few days before the ship was to arrive in New York harbor, he ran out of food. He drank water and did without for a day or so. Then he got so hungry he didn't think he could last. So he scraped together all the money he had left—several coins—and went to a steward in the dining room.

"Excuse me, please," he said. "Is this enough money to buy just a little bit to eat? I've run out of food and I'm very hungry." The steward said, "Sir, you do not need to pay extra to eat in the dining room. Your meals were paid for in the price of your ticket."

I urge you to begin living up to your privileges in God. Jesus Christ paid for them in the price of your passage to heaven!

Blessing, gladness, satisfaction, goodness, and all other spiritual pleasures are yours. *Happy is he that hath the God of Jacob for his help, whose hope is in the Lord his God* (Psalm 146:5).

Chapter Seven

I'M SAFE!

What a special blessing I received not long ago from one of our longtime ministry partners, a dear lady named Doris Ulich. She has been a special friend and supporter of Jack Van Impe Ministries for years and years.

By the way, Jack and I feel such gratitude to all our many partners who are faithful with their prayers and generous financial support to help us proclaim the Gospel via television across America and around the world. As you know, we recently launched a new campaign to again win a million souls to Christ, and we are keenly aware that without your partnership, the scope of our outreach would be limited. Truly, ...*we are labourers together with God...* (1 Corinthians 3:9).

So when Doris phoned the ministry office one day and said she needed to speak to me, I was most interested in knowing what she had to say. As soon as I got the message, I called her back.

She said, "I've just had one of the greatest blessings of my life, and it concerns you and your husband. I couldn't wait to let you know about it."

Doris went on to explain that she has a younger brother who

is mentally challenged. He was born with this condition and grew up with the love and support of his family. He now lives in a facility with other special people like himself, where each individual has his own room, does many things for himself, and may even hold down a job in the community.

...that they might have life...more abundantly
—John 10:10

I'm told that great progress is being made with the mentally challenged. Through medical research and new medications and treatments, their life expectancy has increased from 25 to 45 years! And the widespread support of programs like the Special Olympics have helped build the confidence and self-esteem of these young people while enhancing public awareness of their courage, joy, and value as people.

I know I have been impressed with a couple of these special youngsters who work as sackers in the supermarket where I shop. They are so focused on the job they've been trained to do, and they take such pride in their work. In fact, the day I started writing this article, I stopped by the store and one of these sackers, a young woman, greeted me and said, "I see you on TV...and I like you."

I thanked her and visited with her for a moment. Then, as I was leaving (knowing our telecast was on that evening), I said to her, "I'll see you tonight." She smiled so sweetly and replied, "Yes, I'll see you!"

But I must get back to Doris' story about her brother. She told me that he is a faithful viewer of our "Jack Van Impe Presents" program. He tunes in almost every week and tries never to miss a program. Doris said that often when the two of them would talk on the phone, her brother would say, "I just saw the Van Impes on TV."

"Well, did you enjoy it?"

"Oh, yes," he'd say. "I like Rexella and Dr. Jack 'cause they love Jesus."

Then one stormy night the power went out at Doris' house and she gave her brother a call. "How about I come over and watch the Van Impes with you?"

"Sure," he said, "come on over."

So she went over and watched "Jack Van Impe Presents" with her brother. As the program unfolded that night, she wondered—as she so often had before—just how much of the message he understood and if he personally identified with what was being said. Her main concern was whether or not he'd ever opened his heart to the Lord."

After the telecast was over, she looked over and asked, "Did you enjoy the program tonight?" Her brother nodded his head and said he did. Then she asked, "You know that prayer Dr. Van Impe says at the end—have you ever prayed that prayer with him?"

"Oh, yes," he said, nodding his head vigorously. "I prayed that prayer and I'm safe!" He truly viewed his life from the *Inside Out*.

Isn't that a great statement of faith? I'm so glad Doris blessed me by sharing that wonderful testimony with me.

There is no safety in our world

In this day and age, more people than ever before are searching for safety. They are looking for someplace to hide from the threatening events in our world...the tragedy and turmoil that seems to be everywhere. The Israeli-Palestinian conflict threatens to engulf the whole world in warfare. The struggle against terrorism around the globe goes on. Entire nations in Africa are being devastated by the AIDS virus. Hunger, disease, and political unrest are seething on almost every continent.

Even America has discovered that it cannot escape the dangers and suffering of our world. A great many people have found out the hard way that they couldn't put their trust in riches, with huge investments disappearing almost overnight!

The American Institute of Stress, a Yonkers, New York-based organization, recently reported on its Internet Web site that experts estimate that as many as 75 to 90 percent of all doctor's office visits are for stress-related ailments. And following the awful events of September 11th in New York City, the number of prescriptions written for patients with anxiety and depression increased by a dramatic 25 percent!

Our world is truly coming to the end of the age just prior to the coming of the Lord. We can expect to see things accelerating toward that all-important event. Without question, more and more people will be searching for security, a shield against the trouble of the world.

But God's Word says they will not find it. First Thessalonians 5:3 warns, *For when they shall say, Peace and safety; then sudden destruction cometh upon them, as travail upon a woman with child; and they shall not escape.*

For many years, Jack and I have been privileged to know a "special" young man named Johnny, the son of one of our staff members who has been with the ministry almost from the beginning. Johnny is "safe," too, with very strong faith. I'm telling you, he loves Jesus. Because his trust is in the Lord, he walks through this world without worry or fear, at peace in God's presence.

Sheltered in the arms of God

The great songwriter, Dottie Rambo, expressed the wonderful confidence we can have as children of God when she wrote—
> He walks with me, and naught of earth
> shall harm me, for I'm sheltered in
> the arms of God.

How can you "anchor your soul in the haven of rest" and declare confidently that "in Jesus, I'm safe evermore"?

The Lord made it very clear in Matthew 18:2,3—*And Jesus called a little child unto him, and set him in the midst of them, and said, Verily I say unto you, Except ye be converted, and become as little children, ye shall not enter into the kingdom of heaven.*

Do you have the simplistic faith and trust of a little child...or even a precious "mentally challenged" youngster? Trust in the Lord today. Cast all your cares on Him. Because He will never leave you or forsake you, you can learn to walk through the darkest nights and roughest places, facing whatever may come with your hand in God's hand.

And then you can say, "I'm safe!"

Chapter Eight

WALKING IN MY SHOES

I truly enjoy reading the letters that come to my attention. While our demanding work schedules don't permit Jack and me to see every single piece of correspondence sent to the ministry, we read as many letters from friends and partners as we possibly can to stay in touch with how people are feeling. I especially take delight in letters from children or other "special" mail.

Recently I received a most unusual request from a woman representing a small charitable group dedicated to preventing domestic violence and helping provide a safe, warm environment for victims of abuse. The letter I received requested me to donate...a pair of my shoes!

Shoes? *Used shoes?* Yes, it seems this group collected shoes from celebrities or well-known people and "auctioned" them to donors who made contributions to this most-worthy charitable cause in the name of the person whose shoes they bought. I found myself intrigued by this strange request and the group's novel fund-raising project.

The young woman who wrote to me said she wanted my shoes because she had observed that I had been instrumental in helping people make positive changes in their lives through the love of Jesus, and was dedicated to helping share the Word of God to tens of thousands of people around the world. "You are someone that I am honored to ask to help us," she wrote.

Needless to say, I soon found myself in my closet searching for a pair of shoes to send. I actually ended up sending more than one pair, hoping that the group could find others who'd make a contribution for my shoes. How could I possibly turn down such an unusual request?

As I was looking at my shoes, I couldn't help thinking about all the places those shoes had gone. Places and events flashed into my mind as I held each pair in my hands. In many cases, I actually remembered where I had been and what I had been doing when I wore those shoes.

Some of the shoes had carried me to crusade services in thousands of cities across America and into fifty countries across the world. The blue ones with the bow — I'd worn them on tent and auditorium platforms to sing the Gospel for the Lord. I'd worn these shiny black ones years ago when I conducted on-camera interviews with some of the most interesting and influential men in world politics. The old, worn lace-ups with the scuffs were traveling shoes — I wore them in the ministry van during the long hours we drove from city to city. I wore this pair just last week in the TV studio as we taped the latest "Jack Van Impe Presents" program. The soft "at home" slippers were favorites I wore into my prayer closet to seek God's direction and to intercede for people with needs and troubles.

I soon decided that every pair of shoes had its own story to tell as I reminisced there in my closet. They had carried me through dust and mud, snow and ice. Sometimes they had been soiled and scarred by long, hard roads. At times they had been spotted and stained by my own falling tears. What amazing stories would be told if my shoes could talk.

Beautiful feet

As I stood there, I couldn't help but wonder that if someone slipped on my shoes and let them carry her to where they had taken me, would I be confident or ashamed. "Oh, Lord," I whispered, "I hope my shoes would have a worthy testimony of carrying beautiful feet." As the Prophet Isaiah so eloquently exclaimed, *How beautiful upon the mountains are the feet of him that bringeth good tidings ... that publisheth salvation* (Isaiah 52:7).

Even after I turned off the light and shut my closet door, I kept thinking about shoes. I remembered hearing people over the years say how they wished they could walk in the shoes of some prominent minister or some other person they respected or admired. And I knew that in some cases they would have been disappointed, possibly even disillusioned, if they'd followed in the footsteps of their hero who might not have followed the straight and narrow pathway.

In today's world, we have often seen men and women in public life fail to set good examples. Sports figures who should have taken more responsibility for their influence on admiring young people have disclaimed their position as role models. Top business, military, and political leaders have blatantly violated the principles of truth, honor, and morality and willfully wallowed in cesspools of deceit and degradation. Who would want to wear their shoes?

Treacherous shoes

The failure of mankind is not limited to modern examples. The Bible abounds with stories of individuals who chose to follow perilous pathways. Consider the treacherous shoes of Judas, one of the disciples who followed Jesus. Although he walked in the presence of the Master, heard His teachings, witnessed His miracles, and shared the most intimate moments with our Lord, somewhere along the way Judas obviously began to travel down the wrong road.

I believe Judas lived a double life. The other disciples must have trusted him because, according to the Gospel of John, Judas was the keeper of the bag, or treasurer, for the disciples—but he was also dishonest, pilfering what was entrusted to his care (see John 12:6). And if you will recall, at the Last Supper, when Jesus announced that one of the twelve would betray Him, no one pointed an accusing finger at Judas. Rather, all of them asked, "Is it I?"

At one time, Judas had the opportunity to share in Christ's ministry. Who knows where he might have gone and what God might have accomplished through him? But Judas's shoes carried him into the minefield of money.

When Mary of Bethany anointed Jesus' feet with very expensive ointment, Judas indignantly demanded of the Lord why He allowed such waste when the ointment could have been sold and the money given to the poor. He said this not because he cared about the poor, John tells us, but because he had become a thief and coveted the three hundred pence that might have been put within his care.

And it was money that drove him to betray Jesus. Judas went to the chief priests and asked, "What will you give me if I deliver Him to you?" (see Matthew 26:15). The sandals of Judas made a wrong turn and became shoes of treachery.

Over the centuries, many have despised Judas for his deliberate treachery, betraying Jesus to the lynch mob with a kiss. But how many still wear shoes like his — treacherous shoes, lying shoes, cheating shoes? How many shoes are filled with feet that go to church on Sunday and to the house of the devil for the rest of the week? How many betray the Lord even today, perhaps not for thirty pieces of silver, but through other forms of selfishness and greed? Their treacherous footwear propels them to wrong places to do wrong things that betray Jesus day after day.

I heard a heartbreaking story of a woman who felt she had to get a divorce after thirteen years of marriage. She had two beautiful children who didn't lack for anything. Her husband was a successful businessman who provided an affluent lifestyle, with a nice house, beautiful clothes, and expensive cars. What was the problem? She discovered that on his lunch hour several times a week, her husband would leave the office and visit prostitutes. Betrayal! Deceit!

Here was a man who seemed to have it all. Respect of colleagues. Prestigious neighborhood. All the trappings of prosperity. But he couldn't keep from wearing the shoes of treachery. And they took him down the slippery slopes to destruction.

Wandering shoes

Jesus himself told the story of the prodigal son, the young man who left his father's house with his inheritance and wasted it on riotous living in a far country (see Luke 15). He may have been led astray by the lure of popularity and the approval of the crowd. He thought he could buy satisfaction and fulfillment with money. He kept looking for a good time, taking pleasure in the things of the world. And all the while, his wandering shoes took him farther and farther away from his father.

Perhaps the prodigal son's intent was not as evil and treacherous as Judas's, but his self-centered shiftlessness was destructive, nonetheless. He didn't stop until he hit bottom. When he had wasted everything he had and lost the adulation of the crowd, he ended up in the pigpen, his shoes battered and worn, ruined by the slop and the slime of the swine.

In desperation, he started back to his father's house, hoping to become a servant so he could at least have room and board. But his father had never given up on him. He had kept on looking down the road, waiting for his wandering son to come home. And one day he saw a familiar figure. He didn't look the same as when he had left. This man was dirty, dejected, humiliated, broken, smelly, and at the end of himself. But he was still beloved! And the father went running to meet him, embraced him, and wept over him with tears of joy and jubilation.

"Bring a clean robe for my son," he cried. "Prepare a bath for him. Put a ring of gold on his finger. Cook a banquet feast.

Tell everybody to come help me celebrate! My son who was lost has come home!"

"Oh," said the father, "one more thing. Throw away these worn-out, run-over, dirty, pig-pen smelly, wandering shoes. Bring new shoes to put on his feet. My son is home at last!"

Have you made some wrong turns in your life? Has your wandering taken you farther and farther away from the Father's house? Have you wasted what you have been given, and ended up in a low and shameful place?

Move toward the Father

It's not too late for you. You can go back to the Father. Get rid of your wandering shoes and make your way back to the place from which you started. Don't worry about what you will say when you get there. Don't be afraid of whether He will receive you or not. The minute you start moving toward Him, the Father will see you and come running to meet you, arms outstretched, words of welcome streaming from His lips, tears of joy pouring from His eyes. He will wash you and restore you. He will dress you in new robes of righteousness. He will prepare the fatted calf and call all the family to welcome you home. He'll put a golden ring upon your hand to show that you belong to Him.

And He'll put new shoes upon your feet!

If we had the time and space, we could find many other examples from God's Word of individuals whose shoes went astray. We could examine Jonah, who ran from God. We could study Peter, whose wishy-washy sandals walked on the water with Jesus...and ran to hide in the alley when Jesus was being condemned to die. There are so many more. A common thread in every example would be that going away from God and following the footsteps of any man is risky. Only as we look to the Lord do we find an Example and Guide who will never fail. The only safe path we can follow is in His steps!

Well did the psalmist declare, *Thy word is a lamp unto my feet, and a light unto my path* (Psalm 119:105). I'm told that in olden days, some people actually attached little lamps to the toe of each of their shoes, which freed up their hands to carry a load. As they walked into the darkness, the little lamps gave out just enough light for one more step.

Illumination of dark roads and sidewalks is not such a great problem anymore. With electric streetlights and battery-powered flashlights, it's fairly easy to see where we're going no matter which direction we go. But the darkness in men's hearts and minds is as great as ever. Only in the Word of God can we find the source of light that chases away the shadows and illuminates the right road to follow. If we seek — and respond to — the guidance of the Holy Spirit, we will find our feet following *in the paths of righteousness for his name's sake* (Psalm 23:3). And we will discover by experience that *the steps of a good man are ordered by the Lord* (Psalm 37:23). Then and only then will we view life from the *Inside Out*.

Walking unashamed

After a while, I picked out some of my shoes and sent them to the charitable organization that had requested them. But the lesson the Lord brought to my mind when I received that request is with me still. I don't think I'll ever forget it. My prayer is that the Lord will help me to live my life in such a way that if anyone ever put on my shoes and walked where I had walked, she would not be ashamed. If she should go where I had been, may her path have led her close to Jesus, Whose I am and Whom I serve.

I recall a little children's Sunday school song that says:

> *Oh, be careful little feet where you go,*
> *Oh, be careful little feet where you go,*
> *For the Father up above is looking down in love,*
> *So be careful little feet where you go.*

Every morning now when I put on my shoes, I find myself whispering a prayer. "Lord, where are You going to lead me today? What opportunities for ministry will I find on my pathway?"

One of these mornings very soon, a glad new day will dawn

and all of God's children will be going home. What a glorious day that will be. I can hardly wait to see my Lord and Savior and rejoice in His presence. I have many beloved family members and friends who are already on the other side that I want to see again. And I can't even begin to imagine how beautiful heaven must be. At some point, I'm sure I'll want to explore the glorious abode where all of the redeemed will live for eternity.

What will it be like? I won't know until I get there. I'm only sure that it will be wonderful. Do you know what I think might happen? In the words of a beautiful old spiritual—

> *I got shoes, you got shoes,*
> *All God's children got shoes!*
> *When I get to heaven,*
> *'gonna put on my shoes and*
> *shout all over God's heaven.*

Chapter Nine

ARE YOU IN CONTACT WITH YOUR SPIRIT GUIDE?

He will guide you into all truth!

We're hearing so much in this day about the New Age Movement and how we should be in contact with our "other self" through our "spirit guide." These concepts are being taught in our public schools, even at the lower grade levels. Misguided, deceived individuals are teaching our innocent children about transcendental meditation, yoga, and the spirit world.

Numerous celebrities, such as Shirley MacLaine, Linda Evans, and John Denver, have publicized their involvement with such fearsome ancient spirit guides as Ramtha, Spectra, and Lazirus, who supposedly possess supernatural knowledge and can assist them in making important decisions and choices.

The truth is that most of the spirits out there are not holy. It is vitally important to recognize this fact. Sadly, too many people do not realize that when they participate in activities like "channeling," trances, seances, etc., they are opening themselves up to all kinds of demonic spirits. Often, people actually give themselves over to evil spirits, with tragic results.

Our Guide

As Christians, our Spirit Guide lives within us. Your *body is the temple of the Holy Ghost which is in you* (1 Corinthians 6:19). Therefore, if our Spirit Guide is within us, we have no need to go outside ourselves for guidance as others suggest. He is all we need.

Howbeit when he, the Spirit of truth, is come, he will guide you into all truth: for he shall not speak of himself but whatsoever he shall hear that shall he speak: and he will show you things to come (John 16:13).

Imagine, you have access to the greatest Spirit of all—the precious Holy Spirit. You can possess, and be possessed by, the most powerful force in all the universe, the omniscient, omnipresent Spirit of the eternal God. Shirley MacLaine and others talk about their spirit guides being so special because they are ancient. But our Spirit Guide—the Holy Spirit—helped create the world, even man.

Genesis 1:1,2 says, *In the beginning God created the heaven and the earth. And the earth was without form, and void; and darkness was upon the face of the deep. And the Spirit of God moved upon the face of the waters.* So the Holy Spirit was there at the dawn of creation—as a part of the Trinity. He is from the beginning and predates all other spirit guides.

We can have contact with this Holy Spirit and be guided by Him, but first we must possess Him. The only way that can happen is by the illumination of His Word. He must convince us of the truth. John 16:8 says, *And when he is come, he will reprove* [convince] *the world of sin, and of righteousness, and of judgment.* He convinces us that we need Him and guides us to the born-again experience.

Thank God, the Spirit does strive with us and illuminates the truth to us.

Our Intercessor

Not only does the Spirit convince us of our need of Christ, He also creates intercessory thoughts in us. There are times when we don't even know what we need—what is good for us. So many times we may not even know how we should pray or what we should ask for. So we have to join our spirit with the Holy Spirit to seek out God's best plan for our lives. Romans 8:26 says, *Likewise the Spirit also helpeth our infirmities: for we know not what we should pray for as we ought: but the Spirit itself maketh intercession for us with groanings which cannot be uttered.*

There are times when we come to God, praying only for what we want—asking for His approval—instead of seeking His will for our lives. I'm convinced that on those occasions when we come to God, asking selfishly, the Holy Spirit is saying, "No, Father, no." When we do not ask within the will of God, then the Holy Spirit, in His mercy, intercedes for what is best.

As a young bride, I had an experience like this. I wanted a baby so much that I begged God to let me have one. I refused to consider how much a child would have hampered and burdened my calling and ministry, which at that time required me to live "on the road" for months at a time. I avoided thinking about how cruel and unfair my work-load and life-style would be to a helpless, wholly-dependent little one.

Even after I knew that motherhood was not God's will for me, I asked anyway. But the Holy Spirit, in His goodness, interceded for me—for my own good. And now, as I see things clearly from the *Inside Out* and in perspective, that knowledge brings me great comfort.

There may also be times when we experience a yearning for something that is undefined and inexpressible. It's a hunger or yearning we simply can't understand. At times like these, we can join our spirits with the Holy Spirit and let Him create intercessory thoughts within us. Then we can have peace that what is being sought in our behalf is for our good...and will be done. *And this is the confidence that we have in him, that, if we ask any thing according to his will he heareth us: and if we know that he hear us, whatsoever we ask, we know that we have the petitions that we desired of him* (1 John 5:14,15).

Allowing the Holy Spirit to create intercessory thoughts and prayers brings such satisfaction and fulfillment. It goes beyond our understanding or ability to put it into words. It is so beautiful and powerful.

Our Comforter

Then, the Holy Spirit comforts us. *I will not leave you comfortless: I will come to you* (John 14:18).

I love the story about a very sad unbeliever who was seated next to a Christian man on a train. During the trip, the unsaved man began to cry and weep. The believer said to him, "I see you are troubled and sad. Is there some way I can help you?"

The sorrowful man replied, "I've just lost my wife. Our home seems so empty. All I have left to keep me company is her parakeet."

The believer replied, "Well, as a Christian I have the *Paraclete—the* Holy Spirit. He never leaves me. And He will meet your need if you'll allow Him to."

Paraclete, in the Greek, means "comforter" and is the name given for the Holy Spirit. As Christians, we have the constant, unfailing presence of the Holy Spirit to guide and comfort us.

Our Spiritual Gift-giver

The Holy Spirit also controls the spiritual gifts bestowed upon the body of Christ, the Church. *The manifestation of the Spirit is given to every man to profit withal. For to one is given by the Spirit the word of wisdom; to another the word of knowledge... to another faith...to another the gifts of healing... to another the working of miracles; to another prophecy; to another discerning of spirits; to another divers kinds of tongues; to another the interpretation of tongues: but all these worketh that one and the selfsame Spirit, dividing to every man severally as he will* (1 Corinthians 12:7-11).

God gives these gifts to each believer, as He wills. Each of us has been given a very special gift—and the Holy Spirit will guide us into a place of service using the particular gift He has chosen for us. He will also give us power when using that gift.

Peter had the gift of communication—the ability to preach. But after he was filled with the Holy Spirit (see Acts 1:8; 2:4), he not only had the gift but also the fruit... boldness (see Acts 4:13). So the Holy Spirit not only gives us spiritual gifts, He also gives us the ability (fruit) and strength to use them.

Spiritual gifts are not given to hoard for our own benefit or enjoyment. They are given to enable us to minister to others. And the Spirit will provide the opportunity—He will definitely show us our place of service.

I believe there are times, depending on the circumstances, when more than one gift of the Spirit may be exercised through you. A situation may arise where there is no one else to depend on and the Holy Spirit manifests (or works) a particular gift through you to meet a particular need at a particular time. It may be a gift that has never operated in your life before, but when the Spirit puts you in a situation, He will illuminate your mind to meet the need. You will discover that where God guides, He provides.

The Holy Spirit is our Keeper

Not only is our Spirit Guide with us in life, but He remains with us even after death.

Dr. J. Wilbur Chapman relates a beautiful story about how he personally discovered this thrilling truth. He was sitting in his home, reading an address delivered by Dr. Moorhead at a Bible Conference. Dr. Moorhead declared that when one becomes a child of God, the Spirit of God comes in to dwell in that person and will continue in that body until the Resurrection. Even after the human spirit has departed to be with the Lord, the third member of the godhead remains with that body until the Resurrection.

Dr. Chapman said that as he thought about this, he started to cry. He said, "We hitched the horse to the carriage, and my wife and I rode out to a little graveyard where we had buried our firstborn son. As we stood there beside that little grave, we said, Thank You, Lord, for keeping watch.' Immediately the peace of God flooded our souls." He went on, "Later, when I stood by the grave of my mother, again I said, Thank You, Holy Spirit, for staying with Your temple and keeping watch.'"

What a comfort! On the day of Resurrection the Spirit will touch the body with new life, reunite it with the soul, and sweep our triuned body, soul, and spirit to be with God. How amazing and beautiful!

I encourage you today to get in contact with your Spirit Guide. But don't be fooled by the false teachers of the so-called New Age Movement. Satan always has a counterfeit for the real and profitable things In life. He would like to deceive you into listening to his emissaries of evil and guide you into darkness. But he is no match for the real "Spirit Guide"—the Holy Spirit, who will always guide you into all truth. Remember, *Greater is he that is in you, than he that is in the world* (1 John 4:4).

Chapter Ten

DRINKING THE WATER
WE HAVE GIVEN AWAY

Do you ever feel thirsty and dry in your spirit?

Believe it or not, that may be a signal that you need to be pouring out a fresh supply of the water of encouragement and blessing into somebody else's life! Yes, I really mean that we should be giving away the very thing we need. That's what the Bible teaches — Proverbs 11:25 — *he that watereth shall be watered also himself.*

That's not the way of the world, is it? Man's natural inclination seems to be to hoard any commodity that is in short supply — to look out for self first. "Let me get mine first," people say, "and you can make do with what's left."

God has a different plan in providing good things for our lives. The ancient wisdom of Proverbs still seems radical to many people — that in order to get we must give. To be truly happy we must make other people happy. To achieve personal spiritual maturity we must patiently help others find and follow God's plan and will for their lives.

Only as we give do we open the channels of supply from which we receive. People who give much find that they get even more in return (Luke 6:38). And those who don't give what they should, inevitably end up poor — in spirit as well as in material things.

The New Testament echoes the lesson of Proverbs 11. Writing in 2 Corinthians 9, the Apostle Paul declared, *He which soweth sparingly shall reap also sparingly; and he which soweth bountifully shall reap also bountifully* (verse 6).

Givers and takers

God is so good to us — what wondrous blessings He pours into our lives daily. What is our attitude and response to the good things we receive from His hand? Someone has said there are only two kinds of people in the world — givers and takers. Which kind are we? Do we get to give or get to keep?

I heard it said about "takers" that they sit, they soak, and they sour. What a telling — and terrible — description. That certainly is not what God wants for us after we have experienced the miracle of new life when Christ comes into our hearts. God is a giver! The Golden Text of the Bible, John 3:16, says that God so loved that He gave. He gave His only Son as a sacrifice for the salvation of all mankind.

Jesus was a giver, too. All through His earthly ministry He gave of himself to everyone around Him — loving, teaching, healing, delivering, blessing — and through His death He bore the penalty for sin and provided everlasting life to all who receive it. God wants us to give out the water of life to others. And as we water others, we also are watered ourselves

My mother, the giver

My dear, sweet mother is one of the most perfect examples of this great Christian principle. Among the precious memories from my childhood is the recollection of how she loved to prepare wonderful meals to share with others. My brothers and I never had to make an appointment to bring friends home from church for Sunday dinner. She took great joy in welcoming them to our table, and there was plenty for all. As she served the meal, there was a light in my mother's eyes, a special glow on her face

Mother was always sensitive to the needs of others. Often she would bake pies or cakes to share with people in the neighborhood who needed a little uplift or special attention. And she was quick to volunteer her help in the church kitchen when meals were being prepared for a bereaved family or a special dinner was to be part of some ministry activity. She gave generously of her time and efforts.

My mother never had a lot of money. But she was always putting back part of her meager allowance, saving up for something she needed or wanted. Time and again I've seen her quietly and cheerfully give away her savings to some person in trouble or someone with a special need. She was constantly watering the lives of others. And I must say that her life was enriched and watered in return. My mother was always happy.

Then came a time when sickness sapped her strength and made it difficult for her to be as active in doing for others. In my concern, I tried to get Mother to not overdo and wear herself out cooking, baking, and doing for others. "It's time for you to rest more and let someone else do some of these things," I told her.

So Mother tried to cut back and let others carry on the work she did for so long. I think she sensed my concern and didn't want me to worry. But after a while, I noticed a growing sense of sadness and heaviness of spirit in her that I'd never seen before. As I prayed about it, I realized that by asking her to hold back in giving of herself to bless others, I was depriving her of the fulfillment of her ministry — and of being "watered" through giving.

So I called her one day and said, "Mother, do whatever you feel God wants you to do. Don't hold back anymore because of me. I want you to be happy." She didn't say a lot, but from that day on I could sense a change of attitude. Life came back into her eyes, and there was a noticeable brightening of her attitude and outlook.

At this stage of her life — perhaps the winter season — she still takes great joy in watering other people's lives. Her physical strength does not allow her to do all she used to do. But she has found new ways to be sensitive to the guidance of the Holy Spirit. Now she calls people with a word of encouragement, writes personal notes, or sends cards. She has a beautiful ministry of encouragement.

Everyone who knows my mother is blessed as she shares her gifts of love with them. It's so beautiful to see God's Word being fulfilled in her life right before my very eyes! Giving has so enriched her life. As she has used her talents for the benefit of others, she has become so much more beautiful, beloved, and treasured than if she had sat out her life on the sidelines. What a wonderful example her life is to me, as well as others.

Water the lives of others

So many people have latent talent — hidden, underdeveloped potential — which is being wasted. God expects us to use whatever talents we have been given. In the words of a wonderful old gospel song, "If just a cup of water I place within your hands, then just a cup of water is all that I demand."

I believe that when we are entrusted with a talent, God will provide opportunities for us to develop and use it. For example, the pastor may come and ask, "Would you be a Sunday school teacher?" Instead of drawing back and saying, "I can't do that" or "I don't have the time," the better response may be to agree to try. When God gives us a talent and an opportunity, I believe He will empower us to do what He calls us to do. You'll discover that in instructing others you gain knowledge yourself. As you begin to teach a class, you will learn more than anybody. As you "water" your class, you also will be watered!

What kind of watering can has God placed in your hands? What opportunities do you have to pour refreshing, life-giving water into the lives of others?

Not long ago I had lunch with a friend who is an instructor at a local university. This lady, who had lost her husband some years ago, recalled for me the painful difficulties she had gone through and related how empty and alone she felt. Shaking her head sadly, she said, "Rexella, one of the biggest disappointments to me was being abandoned by my Christian friends. I received more comfort and sympathy from the people I worked with than the people I worshipped with!"

Her words were like a knife stabbing my heart. Where were her Christian brothers and sisters in her time of grief and need? Didn't anybody see her pain and loneliness? Didn't anybody care? I asked my friend, "What were your needs from your church friends? What could they have done to comfort and help you?"

"I really didn't need things," she replied. "All I wanted was for someone to be there. I needed someone to call me, come see me, invite me to lunch and provide some fellowship. But after the funeral, everybody just left me alone."

What a sad story. Here was a beautiful lady who just needed some loving concern and attention. Her life was parched and dry — and nobody "watered" it. And because she was not watered, I know that the church people who failed to come to her aid were not watered either! The Bible lesson is very clear. He who waters will also be watered. He who does not water others will not be watered himself! He who sows little will harvest little.

I wish I could say this was an isolated example. But right on the heels of this incident, Jack and I had dinner with some very good friends whose daughter had gone through a divorce. They said almost the same thing as my professor friend. In the midst of the all the pain and hurt their daughter went through, no one from their church had reached out to her. She had received no support, no comfort, no expressions of sympathy. Although not bitter, our friends were bewildered and confused.

Once again I felt a stabbing pain in my heart. Where were God's people when they were needed so desperately? Why couldn't someone — anyone — have been there to listen and pray and love and encourage her during her time of extreme need?

God wants participants — not spectators

Someone once said that Christianity is not a spectator sport. God did not call us to sit in the stands and be onlookers. We are all commissioned to get in the game. The Book of Acts tells us how God anointed Jesus of Nazareth with the Holy Ghost and with power: *who went about doing good, and healing all that were oppressed of the devil; for God was with him* (10:38).

Is God with you? Is the Holy Spirit at work in your life since you received Christ? Do you have God's power within you? Do you go about doing good? Do you reach out to hurting, suffering people with an anointed hand of healing and comfort? Are you pouring fresh water on the dry deserts of those around you?

These are important questions, hard questions. But if we call ourselves disciples of Jesus, people who are like Christ, we must face these questions. The answers must be pleasing to our Lord who has given us all good things.

Recently a friend of mine heard Rabbi Harold Kushner speak at a seminar sponsored by a regional hospital. During his address, this distinguished author and Jewish scholar said that over the years when he was ministering to his local congregation, he often wondered why there didn't seem to be the same involvement and response in the weekly Temple service as in the 12-step group that met in the basement on Tuesday night. The rabbi said that finally he decided the difference was that all the people on Tuesday night were active participants. Too many who attended the worship service were just spectators.

"Too many people in American churches and synagogues have become consumers of worship rather than producers of worship," Kushner concluded. Could he be right? Are there more consumers than producers in the church?

The Spirit-anointed writer of Proverbs spells it out in no uncertain terms. *There is that scattereth, and yet increaseth; and there is that withholdeth more than is meet, but it tendeth to poverty* (11:24). When we sow and work productively, when we give instead of taking, there is a harvest and an increase. If we withhold, or fail to sow, more than we should, our only expectation is poverty.

What should we do? We should wake up and realize that the only water that will quench our thirst is the water we have given away. We probably should underscore Proverbs 11:25 in our Bibles and read it daily until it becomes completely ingrained in our hearts and spirits - *he that watereth shall be watered also himself.*

Help others — and help yourself

I heard an illustration of two men who were trapped in a terrible blizzard, unable to get out of the cold and to a place of safety. One of the men had been injured in the mishap that had trapped them, and was too badly hurt to even move on his own. So all night long the injured man's buddy massaged his legs and helped him to vigorously exercise his arms. "Come on, keep moving," he said over and over. When morning came and rescuers arrived, both men were still alive. By exercising his injured friend to keep him warm, the second man had kept himself warm as well, and both survived the bitter cold of the blizzard. In viewing his situation from the *Inside Out* he did not say, "Why is this happening?" but "How can I make it better?"

Look around you for someone you can help. Is there a hurting, lonely person who needs a friend? Is there a widow who just needs someone to be there? Is there a family in crisis who needs a hand to hold and someone to care?

The Preacher Solomon wrote, *Whatsoever thy hand findeth to do, do it with thy might* - (Ecclesiastes 9:10).

Someone you know is waiting for water. Somebody needs a word of encouragement and a helping hand.

Be available.

Chapter Eleven

⁓

DOES GOD HAVE A "DIGITAL ANGEL"?

Jack and I love ministering on television. Each week when the lights go on and the cameras start rolling, we have the privilege of sharing the Gospel and teaching the message of God's Word to multiplied millions of people. In fact, each "Jack Van Impe Presents" program now reaches more people than we ministered to face to face during all our years of traveling around the world giving the Gospel. Following the 9/11/01 attack on America, we are especially grateful for this avenue of reaching millions each week. We feel the urgency to reach the masses more than ever before.

In addition to broadcasting fifty-two weekly telecasts, which are seen across America and around the world, last year we also produced eight major videos of in-depth analyses of prophetic developments or other biblical studies. For two hours or so, each video explores major news events, prophetic questions, or Bible themes, applying what the Word of God says to practical Christian living.

Besides all the hours of study and prayer required to prepare for those sixty TV appearances, one of my challenges was choosing something appropriate to wear. I always want to look nice, of course, and I try hard to choose garments that are modest, tasteful, and attractive. I believe the clothes I wear are a kind of testimony.

The other consideration, especially on the videos, is to have some variety in color and style. It seems to me that if a viewer watches me for a couple of hours on a video wearing a certain suit, it would be better if I had on something different in the next video.

So when I started to prepare my wardrobe for the last studio production of the year, I was concerned when I couldn't remember what I had worn last. My husband, Jack, has a phenomenal memory, but even he couldn't recall. Like most husbands do when they're trying to play it safe, he threw in a bit of flattery. "It's hard to remember exactly, Rexella," he said, "because you always look great."

I ended up calling my personal secretary and assistant, June, at the office and asking her to look at the last video to see what I had worn. In just a few minutes she called back with the information, which really relieved my mind. I was able to complete my planning with confidence.

Later I was relating this story to my sister-in-law, explaining how good it was to have someone help me out in this way. "You know, Evelyn, one day I won't have to call the office or check with anybody else to find out what I wore or what I did or said. I won't even need to keep a diary, because God has a record book about my life in heaven. He has a record of everything I wear, think, say, or do. Nothing is left out. One day when I stand before Him, He'll open the book and the whole record of my life will be there."

The Word of God makes it absolutely clear that the Lord knows everything about us. Second Chronicles 16:9 says, *For the eyes of the Lord run to and fro throughout the whole earth....* God says, *For mine eyes are upon all their ways...* (Jeremiah 16:17).

And seven chapters later He asks, *Can any hide himself in secret places that I shall not see him?* (Jeremiah 23:24). In the New Testament we read, *...but all things are naked and opened unto the eyes of him...* (Hebrews 4:13).

Because we are literally writing a book every day with our lives, it behooves all of us to make sure that the thoughts and deeds we are recording will not make us ashamed when God opens the book one day (I John 2:28). Never forget that God knows absolutely everything about us, and He doesn't even need a "digital angel" to keep track.

What is a "digital angel"?

Some time ago on our telecast, we talked about an American company that had developed a miniature digital transceiver that can send and receive data and can be continuously tracked by global positioning satellite technology. The company envisioned its "digital angel" as a means of tamper-proof identification for Internet business transactions or a rescue beacon for kidnapped children or missing persons. Other applications might be electronically monitoring the vital signs of "at risk" medical patients or keeping track of criminals under house arrest.

While the developer of this technology envisioned it being used for good and helpful purposes, prophecy scholars immediately recognized that the "digital angel's" capabilities could easily be adapted and utilized as a form of the biblical "mark of the beast" described in Revelation 13:16,17. This tiny microchip could easily be implanted in a person's hand or forehead for identification, authorizing him to "buy or sell."

One reason the negative application of technology like the "digital angel" is so plausible is that through the centuries the devil has often tried to counterfeit the nature and power of God. Do you remember the story in Exodus of Moses and Aaron going before Pharaoh to seek the release of the enslaved children of Israel? When Pharaoh demanded to see a miraculous sign of God's power, Aaron threw down his staff and it became a serpent.

Pharaoh immediately called for his sorcerers and magicians who used evil power to produce a counterfeit copy of the sign—when they threw down their staffs they also became snakes (see Exodus 7:8-12).

The deception continues…and worsens

In our day we have seen fortunetellers trying to foretell the future and duplicate the Word of God's prophets, and witch doctors and shamans trying to copy the healing hand of God to overcome sickness and disease in people's bodies. We have seen New Age practitioners seeking to reproduce various kinds of teachings and practices with spiritual and biblical roots. But their words and deeds were counterfeit, poor imitations of the real thing.

Bible prophecy makes it clear that Satan will continue his deceptions and fake miracles all through the final days of human history. When antichrist comes on the scene, he will perform amazing feats of international diplomacy and power politics, bringing temporary order and peace to a strife-filled, war-torn world.

Then comes a devastating world war that destroys millions of people, and even antichrist is put to death during the horrendous battle of Armageddon (see Daniel 11:45). But wait — he is brought back to life, his body infiltrated and incarnated by Satan himself (see Revelation 13:3).

Notice the parallel to the life and death of Jesus. The Lord came to minister to mankind for a season, then was executed…and came back to life. So naturally the devil will attempt to produce a counterfeit version of those events at the end of the age.

Avoid deception—but don't overcompensate

It is so important that we do not allow ourselves to be deceived. Knowing the truth always sets us free and keeps us free from the lies and counterfeits of the enemy. John 8:32 declares, *And ye shall know the truth, and the truth shall make you free.*

I feel very strongly that too often people—even believers— in their minds and thinking, give Satan more strength and more power than he actually has. He has power, but not *unlimited* power. He is mighty, but he is not *almighty*. And he is not *all knowing*!

Satan cannot read our minds. He does not know our thoughts. He can only hear what we are planning to do if we announce it. Sometimes when I am in prayer, I do not speak aloud the intimacies of my conversation with God. I am careful of what I say.

I have discovered the power of allowing the Holy Spirit to intercede for me. I can allow the Spirit to communicate the deepest secrets of my inner being and cry out to the Father— "Oh, this is so special, so intimate, so powerful. I pray in the Spirit, and I agree with You." When I do this, the devil doesn't even know what I have committed to the Lord and cannot come against me with a specific attack.

Don't misunderstand me. I am not underestimating the enemy. The Bible acknowledges that the devil is "the god of this world" (see 2 Corinthians 4:4). The Apostle Paul also calls him "the prince of the power of the air" (Ephesians 2:2). And he has an army of evil spirits that are sent out to oppose and attack—four-star generals, captains, lieutenants, sergeants, buck privates—all kinds of demonic forces. They relay all earthly messages back to him (Satan). They are his spirit "digital fallen angels."

For we wrestle not against flesh and blood, but against principalities, against powers, against the rulers of the darkness of this world, against spiritual wickedness in high places (Ephesians 6:12). Here's an interesting note—my husband, Jack, in studying the original Greek, has discovered that the term *spiritual wickedness* in the King James version actually should have been translated "spirit wickedness!" Are we not seeing that in our country and our world today?

How can we be victorious in the face of such formidable and evil opposition? How can we live as victorious overcomers and "write" the kind of life book we will be proud for God to see when this life is over?

Starting in the very next verse, we find the answer—*Wherefore take unto you the whole armour of God, that ye may be able to withstand in the evil day, and having done all, to stand. Stand therefore, having your loins girt about with truth, and having on the breastplate of righteousness; and your feet shod with the preparation of the gospel of peace; above all, taking the shield of faith, wherewith ye shall be able to quench all the fiery darts of the wicked. And take the helmet of salvation, and the sword of the Spirit, which is the word of God: praying always with all prayer and supplication in the Spirit...* (Ephesians 6:13-18).

Put on the armor of God

I know this is a familiar passage of Scripture, but if ever we needed to practice the practical points of these verses, it's now! Today, we urgently need the protection and power of the whole armor of God. On 9/11/01, in a few startling, almost heart-stopping moments, millions of Americans (and people all over the world) suddenly realized how vulnerable they were to the attack of the enemy. And even if we don't think we are at risk from the jet-fuel bomb blasts of airliners crashing into buildings or deadly anthrax-laced letters coming into our offices or homes, we are chillingly aware that the enemy is real...and on the attack.

We can stand against the attack only if we are prepared. We can be victorious only when we wrap ourselves in the truth of God's Word and protect our hearts—the vital center of our being—with the breastplate of righteousness. Our right thinking and right living not only please God but protect us from the scarring acids of evil.

Notice that part of the armor—our shoes—involve our witness and testimony. The best way to personally practice the

Gospel is to share it with others! Letting those around you know what you stand for and believe is a good way to be left out of idle conversations and smutty stories. And helping *prepare* for the propagation of the gospel through your financial support of missions outreaches like this ministry's telecasts and literature is also a way to be part of God's work.

I love this next phrase—*above all*—that makes it very clear, doesn't it—*above all.* What is this most important thing? Shield yourself with faith! No matter how the enemy seems to be raging, God is still in control. Have faith. Believe in Him. Put your hand in His hand. Your faith will protect you and actually put out—that's what the word *quench* means—the fiery darts of the devil!

All the rest of the armor is important, too—the helmet of salvation, the sword of the Spirit (which is the Word of God), and praying in the Spirit. So you see, we are not helpless. We do not have to stand on the sidelines and wring our hands in hopeless anguish. There is something we can do. We can be victorious in the face of seemingly overwhelming opposition.

Live for Jesus!

Every hour of every day, our lives can write a new page in the record book God keeps. Every day is a fresh, new page—a new opportunity to overcome the flesh and the devil. Sure we will face temptation...and perhaps even stumble. I still make mistakes from time to time. But if I am faithful to confess the thoughts and actions of my fleshly nature, God is faithful to forgive (see 1 John 1:9). And what God forgives is washed away and erased from the record. It's not in the book.

Oh, I get so thrilled about living for Jesus and enjoying the power and victory He provides. I am excited about what God will do *for* us and *in* us and *through* us in the weeks and months ahead!

Oh, my friend, I encourage you to not be afraid or fearful about what may come. Don't spend any time worrying about the enemy's pseudo *intelligence* like electronic spies or "digital angels" watching and listening. Just live for Jesus—that's what matters.

Remember the undeniable truth of the old gospel song—

Many things about tomorrow
I don't seem to understand,
But I know who holds tomorrow,
And I know who holds my hand.

Chapter Twelve

I WANT TO BE
A CLONE

I entered the "clone zone" on one of our recent "Jack Van Impe Presents" television programs!

As I read several international news headlines and the detailed report about the developing technology of scientific cloning, my mind was racing. I'm sure you are aware of the medical, legal, and religious controversy over the morality of man's newly demonstrated ability to produce perfect clones from the cells of adult mammals

Probably the most famous farm animal in history was Dolly the sheep, produced in 1997 by Dr. Ian Wilmut and his colleagues at the Roslin Institute in Edinburgh, Scotland. She was the first identical offspring cloned from adult cells, with no father.

Then came two calves created by Japanese scientists in 1998. And on March 5, 2000, five little piglets, all identical clones, were created by the British bio-pharmaceutical companies that helped to clone Dolly.

Almost every month, it seems, we're seeing new processes of cloning. This fast-emerging technology is demonstrating that by combining cloning with genetic engineering, animals with therapeutic proteins can be produced. And the progress being made in the field could herald animal-to-human organ transplants in the foreseeable future.

Scientists believe that it may soon be possible to use genetically engineered pigs, which can be produced very quickly, to provide transplants since their organs are about the same size as human organs. Doctors say there are about 68,000 people in the United States and some 50,000 in Europe awaiting donor livers, kidneys, and hearts. Many of them will die before a suitable organ is available for a transplant surgery

In the meantime, doctors, biologists, lawyers, and religious leaders are involved in a storm of debate over thorny moral and ethical issues that could be associated with cloning. How long, for example, before someone clones a human being? As an identical copy of another person, will that being have its own identity...its own soul? For the record, scientists say yes. While science can replicate genes, features, and traits, these research doctors are forthright in acknowledging that they cannot recreate and pass on the soul.

Although Jack and I explored the prophetic significance of this scientific feat on the telecast — certainly it could involve man's "knowledge of witty inventions" spoken of in Proverbs 8:12—I really don't want to get into a discussion of these complicated issues in this article. But one thing is for sure — cloning is not going to go away.

Oh, to be like Jesus!

The thing that gripped my mind and imagination even as I presented the news items on the air about cloning was a compelling desire *to be a clone!* No, I'm not saying that I want to be cloned — absolutely not. But I would like to be an identical copy of my Lord and Savior! What an astounding prospect —

that I should be like Jesus.

On the set that day when we were taping, I almost stopped as the truth came bursting into my mind that Jesus has many, many followers, but too few clones. Yet, we *can* truly become like Him, look like Him, act like Him, minister like Him! It is possible when we receive Christ into our hearts. The Bible says, *Therefore if any man be in Christ, he is a new creature: old things are passed away; behold, all things are become new* (2 Corinthians 5:17).

Not only do we take on all the characteristics of Jesus — His Spirit actually comes to live in us. This means that God himself takes up residence within us. That boggles my imagination and understanding! I believe this is what the Apostle Paul was referring to when he declared, *For to me to live is Christ.*(Philippians 1:21).

Paul also said, *For whom he did foreknow, he also did predestinate to be conformed to the image of his Son...*(Romans 8:29). Let me stress again that being a clone of Jesus is not just a physical thing, but spiritual. The Holy Spirit actually comes to live in and through us, giving us the mind of Christ. Philippians 2:5 says, *Let this mind be in you, which was also in Christ Jesus.*

Now let's consider the awesome implications of being a clone of Jesus on two levels, the outward man and the inward man. People often quote the Old Testament verse that says that *man looketh on the outward appearance, but the LORD looketh on the heart* (1 Samuel 16:7).

The Outward man—reflecting the beauty of Jesus

Thank God that He does, indeed, look beyond our physical faults and weaknesses and recognize our inward desires and intentions to please Him. But to my way of thinking, that does not mean the outward man is not important. I believe the way we look should express and reflect the Lord, too. We have to be very, very careful not to allow our outward appearance to be patterned and influenced by the fashions and passions of the world.

What do people mean when they say that someone "looks like the devil"? It's certainly not a positive reference to a wholesome, modest, healthy, godly kind of beauty.

I believe we should try to fashion our outward appearance in personal hygiene, makeup, grooming, and dress in such a way that people can look at us and think that we look like the Lord. I'm not suggesting that we should be drab or dowdy. I believe our appearance can be attractive and appealing, yet modest and proper. We can present ourselves in a way to express the message of a Christian chorus from a few years ago, that says, "Let the beauty of Jesus be seen in me."

When I go shopping for clothes to wear on television, I pray first. I ask the Lord to help me find and choose attire that will represent Him and be a good testimony. I want to be fashionable without being fashioned by the world. I want to be attractive without being an attraction. I even want my colleagues in the communications world to recognize and appreciate my professionalism in the choices I make.

At the risk of stepping on a few toes, I believe it is high time that we uphold the Word of God with the outward man. There are too many Christians today who don't look like Christians...who seem to try to see how much they can look like the world! But the Bible says, *I beseech you therefore, brethren* [and ladies, too], *by the mercies of God, that ye present your bodies a living sacrifice, holy, acceptable unto God, which is your reasonable service. And be not conformed to this world: but be ye transformed by the renewing of your mind, that ye may prove what is that good, and acceptable, and perfect, will of God* (Romans 12:1-2).

The inward man—expressing Christ's nature

Now, how can we be a clone of our Lord in our inner being? How can we actually have His Spirit so connected with our spirits that our <u>inside</u> man glorifies Him <u>outside</u> in every way? The Bible is filled with instruction we can take to heart, steps we should take to align ourselves with Christ's divine example. Take a look at these powerful New Testament passages—

Let all bitterness, and wrath, and anger, and clamour, and evil speaking, be put away from you, with all malice: and be ye kind one to another, tenderhearted, forgiving one another, even as God for Christ's sake hath forgiven you (Ephesians 4:31-32). Look at the pattern—first, put away the fleshly, hurtful, negative things. I don't believe the Bible would ask us to do this unless it were possible! Then we can be receptive to Christ's Spirit and allow the Holy Spirit to control us and express Christ's nature and attributes through us to others.

The same idea is found in Colossians 3:8-10—*But now ye also put off all these; anger, wrath, malice, blasphemy, filthy communication out of your mouth. Lie not one to another, seeing that ye have put off the old man with his deeds; and have put on the new man*

Also, take a look at Galatians 5:19-21—*Now the works of the flesh are manifest, which are these; Adultery, fornication, uncleanness, lasciviousness, idolatry, witchcraft, hatred, variance, emulations, wrath, strife, seditions, heresies, envyings, murders, drunkenness, revellings, and such like…they which do such things shall not inherit the kingdom of God.*

How do we triumph over these sinful, wicked practices? The Word of God makes it very clear. *Walk in the Spirit, and ye shall not fulfill the lust of the flesh* (verse 16).

If we really allow the Holy Spirit to mix with our spirit, He will convict us of those things and empower us to drive them out. The more we turn to the Bible as our guide, the clearer we will see the path where we ought to go. Jesus is the Word. The more we see Him, the more we will believe the Word and react to it.

My heart is so full of the truth God has laid on my heart. How liberating it is to realize that we can distance ourselves from the world—from worldly attitudes, worldly feelings, and worldly reactions. The anger that seizes us is strictly carnal. The bitterness that we hold onto is strictly carnal. Those things are not of God. They must go as we are transformed, or cloned, into an overcoming being in His likeness.

Abide in the Spirit of God

Wherever you are and whatever your circumstances, you can dwell in the Spirit of God. Step by step, day by day, you can live in Christ's presence and walk in His steps. And as you abide in Him, you will become productive and fruitful. Jesus said, *I am the vine, ye are the branches: He that abideth in me, and I in him, the same bringeth forth much fruit...* (John 15:5).

And what kind of fruit will we produce? Read it for yourself in Galatians 5:22-23—*But the fruit of the Spirit is love, joy, peace, longsuffering, gentleness, goodness, faith, meekness, temperance....* Notice that these are attributes that we can't manufacture ourselves. They have to be lived out through us by the spirit of God. And the only way that can happen is for us to become clones of the Spirit.

That's what God has always wanted for His children. The Old Testament prophet, Ezekiel, cried out the Lord's promise to Israel—*A new heart also will I give you, and a new spirit will I put within you: and I will take away the stony heart out of your flesh, and I will give you an heart of flesh* (Ezekiel 36:26-27).

Have you ever felt like your heart was hard and stony? God will give you a new heart. He will strip away the heart of callused indifference and selfish complacency and put in its place a heart that is tender and sensitive, a heart that beats with divine love and compassion. Your whole life will be renewed by the heart of God—not a physical transplant but an infusion of God himself dwelling within.

Oh, that God would do a new and wonderful work in all our hearts!

Become a clone of the Great Original!

You see, I believe it is possible to be born again and a follower of the Lord and still not be His clone. We can still hold back a part of our being. We can still hang on to some bitterness here and there. We can still demand our own way at times. But we must learn to yield in all things if we really want to be what He wants us to be.

When we reach the point in our relationship with God where the Spirit controls our lives, we will be filled with power to be effective in reaching the lost and witnessing to others. I believe the glow of the Spirit will radiate from us with such light and power that we will not have to go out looking for opportunities to minister. People will be drawn to us.

The Lord knows who He can trust to lift Him up and share His love. When He has made us worthy, He will open the doors of opportunity and flow through us to draw all men to Him. He is the way, the truth, and the life. He is the Great Original!

Oh, I want to be His clone!